Harlan, David,
    1942-

    The clergy and
the Great Awakening
in New England

DATE DUE

NOV 2 4 1988			
JAN 0 4 1990	SEP 30 2005		

The Clergy and the Great
Awakening in New England

Studies in
American History and Culture, No. 15

Robert Berkhofer, Series Editor
Director of American Culture Programs
and Richard Hudson Research Professor of History
The University of Michigan

Other Titles in This Series

The Clergy and the Great Awakening in New England

DISCARDED

by
David Harlan

umi
RESEARCH PRESS

Produced and distributed by
UMI Research Press
an imprint of
University Microfilms International
Ann Arbor, Michigan 48106

Library of Congress Cataloging in Publication Data

Harlan, David, 1942-
    The clergy and the Great Awakening in New
England.

    (Studies in American history and culture ; no. 15)
    Originally presented as the author's thesis, University
of California, Irvine, 1979.
    Bibliography: p.
    Includes index.
    1. Great Awakening. 2. Clergy—New England—
Attitudes. 3. New England—Church history.   I. Title.
II. Series.

BR520.H33 1980   280'.4'0974   80-24012
ISBN 0-8357-1097-1

Contents

Abbreviations

MHS   Massachusetts Historical Society, Boston.
ANTS   Andover-Newton Theological Seminary, Newton, Massachusetts.
AAS   American Antiquarian Society, Worcester, Massachusetts.
DCL   Dartmouth College Library, Hanover, New Hampshire.

For my mother and father
and in memory of my brother.

Acknowledgments

I want to thank Alan Rogers of Boston College, who has taught me, helped me and encouraged me for a long time. I also want to thank Jean Lave of the University of California, Irvine, who has been to me a teacher, a friend and a visible philosophy. Rachel Bernstein read endless epistolary ravings about Old Calvinism, took time away from her own work to read mine, and gave me encouragement and valuable suggestions. Jack Diggins, also of the University of California, Irvine, read nearly all of these chapters and saved me from innumerable blunders and embarrassments. Chris Rutledge helped me with the Massachusetts Archives, the Ezra Stiles Papers and the Journal of the Massachusetts House and, not least, prepared the index for this book. Finally, I want to express my gratitude to David, Anna and Sallie.

Introduction

"The common belief that we gain 'historical perspective' with increasing distance seems to me utterly to misrepresent the actual situation. What we gain is merely confidence in generalizations which we would never dare make if we had access to the real wealth of contemporary evidence."

Otto Neugebauer, *The Exact Science of Antiquity* (1952)

To Jonathan Edwards, the Great Awakening presented itself as the most significant event in history. He called it "the more glorious of any work of God whatsoever" and likened its significance to the creation of the world itself. Its success promised to "make New England a kind of heaven upon earth."[1]

In such a cataclysmic event there could be no neutral ground, no passive bystanders, no indifferent spectators, no "neuters" as Edwards called them. "In the day of battle, when [the] two armies join, there is no such thing for any present as being of neither party; all must be on one side or the other."[2]

In one sense, these words are hortative; they were meant to spur the moderates, the fence-sitters, the "neuters" into commitment. "*There is a necessity* of being either for or against."[3] (My emphasis.) But they were also meant to be descriptive. Later in the same book Edwards described the New England ministry as divided "into two armies, separated and drawn up in battle array, ready to fight one with another." Again in 1743 he wrote that the Awakening had cut the clergy in two and "raised a wall between them up to heaven, so that one party is very much out of the reach of all influence of the other."[4]

These are the perceptions of a man engaged in struggle. The sure knowledge of the meaning of events, the attempt to incite commitment, the perception of polarization, all suggest an ideologue and activist mentality. The remarkable thing is this: Edwards' contention that the Awakening divided the ministry into opposing "armies" has been accepted by historians ever since as an objective assessment. Edwin

Gaustad, in what is undoubtedly the most widely read survey of the Awakening in New England, repeats Edwards' description of opposing armies *verbatim*. Alan Heimert, in *Religion and the American Mind*, speaks of "the fundamental cleavage between rationalists and evangelicals" and asserts that "there were in substance only *two* parties on the American religious scene in the period after the Great Awakening." In *Valley of Discord*, Paul Lucas repeats Edwards' description of the Awakening as a "revolution" and contends that "the unity of the clergy disappeared in the battle of new lights and old lights." James Schmotter speaks of "the theological schism" wrought by the Awakening and asserts that "for the first time in the eighteenth century, pastors no longer spoke the same language; the ministerial consensus had ended." Cedric Cowing, in *The Great Awakening and the American Revolution*, claims that the revivals left the New England clergy "badly divided." Historians have quarrelled about the extent of the social divisions opened up by the Awakening; but all have agreed with Richard Bushman's assessment that "the Awakening polarized opinion" among the New England clergy.[5]

Edwards believed that the Great Awakening divided the New England clergy against itself; he also saw the Awakening as a "battle of ideas," a struggle between Arminianism and Calvinism. In *A Faithful Narrative*, his description of the revival at Northampton in 1735, Edwards claimed that that revival had been precipitated by "the great noise that was in this part of the country about Arminianism." This seemed to Edwards "a very threatening" development; he tells us that the friends of vital piety "trembled" with fear, lest they be swallowed up by this corrupt heterodoxy. Edwards responded with "a sermon concerning Justification by Faith alone," which, according to his own judgment, sparked the revival in Northampton and "overruled [Arminianism] for the promoting of religion."[6] Thus the revival assumed, in his mind, the shape of a struggle between two clearly defined theologies.

He saw the revivals of the early 1740s in exactly the same terms. In *Distingishing Marks*, the revivals' critics are accused of "dislik[ing] the present work because it supports and confirms some principles [i.e., Calvinism] which they have not yet embraced, and against which such prejudices hang about their minds, as they cannot easily shake off. For 'tis certain these fruit do not grow on Arminian ground." And two years later, in *Thoughts Concerning the Revival*, he declared that the Awakening would "entirely overthrow" Arminianism. "Now is a good time for Arminians to change their opinions," he warned, "for the Lord hath spoken good concerning Israel."[7]

This perception, too, has shaped all subsequent treatment of clerical responses to the Great Awakening. Virtually every commentator upon the intellectual history of the Awakening has elevated the debates of the 1740s to the highest level of abstraction, to a conflict between Liberalism and Calvinism, enlightenment and piety, reason and faith. Gaustad describes the conflict as nothing less than a crisis of Western thought itself: "on the one hand the forces of reason, clarity, humanism, logic, liberalism, naturalism, and modernity are deployed. Against these time-honored stalwarts stand the ranks of revelation, mystery, theism, emotion, conservatism, supernaturalism, and medievalism."[8] This interpretation is so typical as to make further examples superfluous; it shapes and colors virtually every interpretation of intellectual developments during and after the Great Awakening.

Moreover, in most treatments of the Awakening, the intellectual drama is seen through the theological and ecclesiastical spectacles of men like Edwards and Charles Chauncy, who are assumed (though never demonstrated) to have been spokesmen for their respective "armies." "Thus," according to Gaustad, "the battle began in Oriental fashion, with the mightiest warriors dueling first (the melee would come later)."[9]

Thus, too, the standard practice of reconstructing the personnel of these opposing armies from the subscription lists for Edwards' and Chauncy's respective publications. If a minister subscribed to Edwards' *Some Thoughts Concerning the Revival*, he is taken for a friend of the Awakening—and, *ipso facto*, a friend to revelation, mystery, theism, emotion, conservatism, supernaturalism, and medievalism; conversely, if a minister's name is found on the subscription list for Chauncy's *Seasonable Thoughts*, he is assumed to have been a critic of the revivals and committed to reason, clarity, liberalism, and the rest. This procedure, and the assumptions which underlie it, inform Clifford Shipton's biographies of Harvard graduates, Cedric Cowing's *The Great Awakening and the American Revolution*, Harry Stout's analysis of clerical alignments during the Awakening, and other works.[10] Almost without exception, the intellectual history of the Great Awakening is written as the ideologues saw it: as a conflict that drew the clergy into opposing armies, each bearing aloft the standard of one of the strains of thought that the Puritan synthesis had formerly held in precarious balance.

One should not underestimate either the attraction or the value of this interpretation. It enables us to see sense and meaning where most of those immersed in the revivals saw only a swirl of confusion; it allows us to identify the Great Awakening as a critical episode in the evolution of American religious thought and to see its significance for later developments; and it connects events in America with developments in all of Western Christendom. By pruning away the uncertainty and ambiguity that gripped the minds of men less perceptive than Edwards and Chauncy, we can see what was at stake and what were the consequences; we can see, in short, how "the past flowed through the event and became the present." Edwards and Chauncy, after all, did articulate the two strains of Puritan theology that have shaped American religious thought ever since.[11]

But we can see consequence only at the expense of context. Edwards and Chauncy represented, respectively, the strains of piety and reason that came to independent fulfillment in the nineteenth century. In this sense, they and their followers were the winners. But what about the losers, the "neuters" against whom Edwards vented his contempt, the moderates who tried to steer a middle course through the turmoil of the Great Awakening? There are not two parties engaged in the struggle, but three: the New Light Calvinists who followed Edwards; the Old Light Liberals clustered around Chauncy; and in the middle, a third group, whom Samuel Mather of the Second Church in Boston called "Regular Lights." Mather thought that this third group, standing between the New Lights and the Old Lights, comprised the great majority of New England clergymen.[12] That is impossible to verify. But their numbers are less important than their self-appointed task: to occupy the middle-ground, aligning themselves neither with New Lights nor Old Lights, celebrating neither the charms of reason nor the seductions of piety, defending both the Great Awakening and the Half-Way Covenant.

The Old Calvinists, as the present study calls this middle-of-the-road group, were not analytically minded theologians. Rather than cleansing inherited orthodoxy of the inconsistencies and contradictions it had accumulated over the preceding century, they sought only to extend that barnacle-laden theology into the middle of the eighteenth century and beyond. They were motivated not by the attractions of consistent theology but by the vision of clerical unity. And they were willing to compromise their convictions in order to achieve their vision.

Consider the case of Ebenezer Parkman, minister of the First Church at Westborough from 1724 until his death in 1782. In both his theology and his ecclesiology, Parkman was orthodox. He welcomed Jonathan Edwards' *Original Sin* when that tome appeared, and during the Awakening he invited both Gilbert Tennent and George Whitefield to come to Westborough and preach from his pulpit. In 1745, when the Marlborough Association of Ministers, of which he was a member, proposed a memorial protesting Whitefield's return, Parkman argued against it and defended the revivals Whitefield had touched off on his first visit.[13] By all accounts he was, as he declared himself in 1743, "a Cordial friend to ye Work of God" then sweeping across New England.[14]

But consider the letters he wrote to Andrew Eliot and to William Cooper on 14 July 1743. In May of that year a group of Old Light ministers had convened at Boston and issued a proclamation condemning the Awakening.[15] Two months later, on 8 July, a number of New Lights gathered in the same town and produced a counter-proclamation defending the revivals.[16] When Parkman learned of this second gathering he wrote a letter to Cooper, the New Light minister in Boston, in which he expressed himself "as being in grateful acknowledgement of ye glorious work of God in Reviving Religion in ye land, *and* against ye disorders which have at ye same time been manifest among us."[17] On the same day — 14 July — he wrote to Andrew Eliot expressing his "grief and sorrow" at the division of clerical opinion exhibited by the two proclamations.

> It cuts me inwardly when I view the indubitable Consequences. Did some sober Gentlemen before regrett that anything at all was done at ye former i.e., May Convention? And did it look necessary to Assemble again to correct ye misconduct and supply ye defects of ye first Attempt? Verily, I have misgivings that we shall too soon find reason to wish that there had been neither of these meetings.[18]

Or consider the example of John Hancock, pastor of the First Church in Lexington from 1698 until 1752. Like Parkman, he welcomed the Great Awakening. At the zenith of its impact he brought nearly eighty new converts into his Lexington church.[19] But also like Parkman, and unlike Edwards or Chauncy, he sought to moderate and soften rather than delineate and sharpen differences of opinion. Thus he greeted the July proclamation with what he called "An Expostulatory and Pacifick Letter." "The minds of many are unhappily leavened with Prejudice already against their faithful pastors," he wrote. "We need not forward their afflictions." Rather than attacking the Old Lights and "exposing their Nakedness," he thought it would have been better "to have silently covered it with a Mantle of Charity."[20]

From the perspective of the nineteenth and twentieth centuries these efforts to preserve New England's Middle Way failed. After the Revolution, Old Calvinism suffered a lingering death and by 1820 it had everywhere expired. But from the perspective of the second and third quarters of the eighteenth century, the Old Calvinists seemed everywhere successful. By 1750 revivalists like Gilbert Tennent and James Davenport had recanted, and former Liberals like Ezra Stiles of the Newport Second Church had warmed their rationalism with an infusion of piety.[21] If Separatist churches proliferated in the early 1740s, they virtually disappeared in the early 1750s; if Anglican and Baptist churches multiplied in the wake of the revivals, they nowhere grew as fast as the orthodox churches. When Edwards abandoned the Half-Way Covenant in 1750, he was followed by virtually no one, even in his own Connecticut Valley; when Chauncy privately abandoned Calvinism for Universalism in the 1750s, he kept it a secret from all but his closest friends.[22] As Stiles declared at the convention of New England ministers in 1760, "we are and continue united in faith and fellowship." We ought to "rejoice" he told his colleagues, "that we are so well agreed in purity of doctrine and worship."[23]

In his book *The New England Mind From Colony to Province*, Perry Miller described early American religious history as a process of "declension," a decline of orthodoxy in the face of eighteenth-century liberalism. This dialectic of orthodoxy (or Calvinism), liberalism (or Arminianism), and emerging pluralism has dominated much of the literature on our religious history. But there have always been voices of dissent. As early as 1912 Francis Christie charged that New England liberalism was a "myth," conjured up by George Whitefield's "rash and unwarranted aspersions" against the New England clergy. Robert Pope made the same point in 1970: "The process which historians have labelled declension is nothing more than the maturation of a sectarian movement." In his biography of Ezra Stiles, Edmund Morgan called New England liberalism a "bogy man" and contended that by the middle of the eighteenth century even the most advanced of New England divines had not yet escaped the confines of orthodox theology. Conrad Wright developed this view more fully in *The Beginnings of Unitarianism in America*. And in a 1968 article entitled "The Myth of 'Arminian-Calvinism'" Gerald Goodwin repeated all of these charges and contended that historians have mistaken the rhetoric of eighteenth-century controversy for a description of eighteenth-century reality. In fact, New England Arminianism was simply a term of reprobation hurled by various factions against one another.[24]

Some of the more dispassionate contemporaries thought the same. In 1726, just nine years before Jonathan Edwards described the "great noise" about Arminianism, Cotton Mather wrote that in all of New England he could not find a single Arminian. Thirty-four years later Ezra Stiles said that he could perceive no "real difference" between the New Lights and the Old Lights "in their opinions respecting the fundamental principles of religion. I may be mistaken," he admitted, "but their different manner and phraseology in explaining the same principles appears to me to be their chief difference." This was in 1760, when the intensity of the conflict generated by the Great Awakening had largely subsided. But even in 1745, when the embers of that controversy were still glowing, Samuel Niles of Braintree admitted that "our present controversy is not about the fundamental points of religion," and explained that "if at any time it has been proved against any minister, that his doctrine or life is not according to the Gospel, he has by our constitution been removed from his ministry."[25]

The point here is that Edwards allowed his own penetrating perception of the issues at stake in the Great Awakening to mislead him into thinking that others saw things as clearly as he did. But most New England clergymen lacked either the inclination or the ability to see abstractions as clearly as Edwards saw them. To men like Samuel Niles, Samuel Mather, Ezra Stiles and a host of others, the conflict was more fluid, less sharply defined, certainly less abstract. Far from presenting a choice between Calvinism and Arminianism, enlightenment and piety, reason and faith, the Great Awakening merely presented them with a problem: how to take advantage of this welcome freshening of religion with the least possible disruption to their theology and to the organization of their ecclesiastical polity. For this reason, factional align-ments within the ministry, as the historian David Hall has recently pointed out, were "fluid, temporary (in their widest dimensions), and partial."[26]

The description of the Great Awakening as a contest between the stark, clearly defined, theological alternatives of Calvinism and Liberalism is clearly inadequate and misleading. The present study does not pretend to offer an alternative. But it does seek to modify the prevailing interpretation by describing the response of those ministers who occupied a middle-ground between the New Lights and the Old Lights. The distinctive feature of these Old Calvinists was their attempt to embrace the revivals without abandoning the compromises of inherited theology—most particularly and importantly, without abandoning the Half-Way Covenant. The first chapter examines the distribution of ecclesiastical power in Massachusetts and Connecticut before the Great Awakening. It begins by asking whether the clergy really possessed the power often attributed to them by historians, and concludes that they did not, that in virtually every area of church governance the laity reigned supreme. The second chapter examines the contradiction between the clergy's emerging self-consciousness—its emerging consciousness of itself as a profession—and its realization that the ecclesiastical polity of New England was controlled by laymen. This contradiction determined, to a very large extent, the Old Calvinists' ambivalent response to the Great Awakening, which is the subject of Chapter 3. Chapters 4 and 5 describe the theological and ecclesiastical thought of the Old Calvinists in the post-Awakening period. Chapter 6 examines the mechanisms by which this ministerial consensus was fashioned and maintained, and Chapter 7 describes the relationship between that consensus and the clergy's response to the imperial crisis of the 1760s and 1770s.

The Context of Religious Moderation:

Part I

1

Ministerial Professionalism and the Distribution of Ecclesiastical Power Before the Great Awakening

Most historians believe that the Great Awakening represented a conflict between extreme opposites: between formalism and enthusiasm, reason and piety, Arminianism and Calvinism, Old Light and New Light. The intensity of this conflict is thought to have shattered the old Puritan Synthesis and opened the way to a newer, more pluralistic and therefore more American theology and ecclesiology. The Great Awakening was thus a crucial event—some say *the* crucial event—in the transit from Puritan to Yankee.[1]

However, few contemporaries would have agreed with this analysis. To most New England clergymen, the revivals appeared not as an intellectual duel between Calvinism and Arminianism, but as a problem: how to participate in and take advantage of this long prayed-for freshening of the religious impulse, while subduing its enthusiast and antinomian tendencies.

Consider the case of Samuel Mather. Mather was minister of the Boston Second Church from 1732 until 1741. In his ministry he combined a liberal theology with an almost obsessive fear of ministerial tyranny. This was an unusual compound that probably accounts for the ambivalence with which he greeted the revivals in 1739. But whatever the source of his ambivalence, it was an attitude/posture that Mather thought he recognized in a good many of his colleagues. Most New England ministers, he told a friend in 1741, were neither Old Lights nor New Lights, but "Regular Lights," men who "understand the power and danger of revivalism."[2]

Other New England clergymen reported the same tripartite division within the ministry. Surveying the ecclesiastical situation from his pulpit in the Newport, Rhode Island, Second Church, Ezra Stiles estimated that of the four hundred and twenty Congregational clergymen established in

New England in 1743, only one hundred and thirty could possibly be called New Lights, "and of these only thirty violent." On the other side, only thirty-eight of the four hundred and twenty New England ministers aligned themselves with the Old Lights.[3]

I

We know very little about the ministry in the eighteenth century. We know a lot about eighteenth-century theology, and even more about the lives of ordinary people in that century, but very little about the men who mediated between the two: the ministers who preached their watered-down Calvinism to New England's increasingly disinterested inhabitants. We have no study of the ministry in the colonial period to match Willard Hurst's study of the legal profession, or Richard Shyrock's work on colonial medicine, or Bernard Cohen's study of colonial science. We do have a superb history of the New England ministry in the seventeenth century, and another covering the first half of the eighteenth century, both of recent origin. But aside from a few scattered journal articles and Ph.D. dissertations, this completes the bibliography on the colonial ministry. As a recent student of the subject reported, "The New England clergy as a social sub-group has been almost completely ignored."[4]

The literature we do have revolves around a single theme: the development of the ministry as a profession. James Schmotter argues that beginning with the revocation of the Massachusetts charter in 1689 the New England clergy became increasingly alarmed by the apparent secularization of colonial society. Their response took the form of "professionalism," which, he says, "represented a significant innovation in the religious thought of New England." This emergent professional self-consciousness consisted of a heightened concern with the qualifications, responsibilities, expectations and goals of the profession, with the deference expected from laymen, and with salary problems. "After 1692 the ministry became an organized, self-conscious special interest group."[5]

Schmotter surveys the literature produced by this emergent professionalism, discusses relations between ministers and magistrates and the character of ministerial careers, and then focuses on three events that he thinks played a central role in shaping the character and fate of ministerial professionalism: the failure of the Proposals of 1705 (which would have established ministerial associations throughout Massachusetts, and invested them with certain judicial powers), the smallpox epidemic of 1721-1722 (which revealed for the first time an extensive, anti-clericalism among Boston's inhabitants and consequently gave additional impetus to the movement for professionalization), and the Great

Awakening (which Schmotter interprets as an upsurge of anti-ministerial feeling that all but destroyed the budding professionalization movement). In the end, professionalism was self-defeating, for it alienated the ministers' only source of income and support: the laity. "The clergy's importance in New England decreased not because ministers paid too-little attention to their calling, but because they paid too much."[6]

This argument is made more explicit and greatly extended in J. William T. Youngs' *God's Messengers: Religious Leadership in Colonial New England, 1700-1750*. In the first decade of the eighteenth century, ministers began to display what he calls "congregational clericalism," i.e., a "courtly" view of ministerial authority and an ever-expanding range of power and prerogative. Functions that in the seventeenth century had involved a close cooperation between ministers and laymen were, in the eighteenth century, increasingly dominated by the clergy. These included selection and examinations of ministers, ordinations, baptisms, admission to communion, and church discipline.

The capstone of these aggrandizing developments was the expansion of ministerial associations. Youngs believes that previous historians have misunderstood the significance of these associations. The Proposals of 1705 had urged the establishment of ministerial associations throughout Massachusetts and, arising from them, standing councils that would have exercised a limited, Presbyter-like dominion over the particular churches. The Proposals were rejected by the General Court, but Youngs thinks that defeat "was something other than it seemed," for associations suddenly sprang up everywhere, like mushrooms in the night.

> Although never formally recognized by the provincial government, these groups soon exercised many of the functions proposed for associations, and even for standing councils, under the Proposals of 1705.[7]

Thus, he argues, the associations gradually came to direct the selection of new ministers and examine their credentials and qualifications, to advise ministers on problems with their individual congregations, to supervise disputes between clergy and laity, and generally to make the important decisions about ecclesiastical matters within their neighborhoods. "Thus the Proposals of 1705, far from marking the height of association efforts in Massachusetts, was but an aspect of a movement toward greater clerical cooperation and control that continued despite the 'defeat' of 1705."[8]

And like Schmotter, Youngs believes that this incipient pro-fessionalism was self-defeating; rather than stemming the process of secularization and fragmentation, it gave those tendencies an added impetus by transforming the ministry into simply another faction pleading for its own self-interest. And also like Schmotter, Youngs argues that it was the Great Awakening that administered the final blow to ministerial professionalism. Populist-minded New Lights attacked clerical presumption and ministerial associations, and in the end they forced the clergy to abandon such pretensions and to recognize that whatever security they might acquire could only come from the voluntary support of their own parishioners. Had the revivals of the 1740s not undercut this incipient clericalism, Youngs believes that the Congregational clergy might well have developed all the hierarchical attitudes and trappings of the Anglican clergy.[9]

There is a great deal of truth to these arguments. The clergy did develop and enunciate an increasingly professional conception of their role in the years between the revocation of the Massachusetts charter and the Great Awakening. But even before the Awakening, this incipient professionalism was challenged by a number of clergymen. Both Schmotter and Youngs ignore this critical literature. Schmotter contends that during the 1720s and 1730s "more and more ministers all across New England openly identified with the profession's cause" and that "they chose to listen only to the self-praise of professional spokesmen."[10] Similarly, Youngs argues that, in the early eighteenth century, New England clergymen adopted the values of ministerial professionalism "with near unanimity."[11] But the role of the ministry was an extremely touchy and contentious subject that continued to divide clergymen throughout the first half of the century. By focusing only on one side of these debates and contentions, Schmotter and Youngs exaggerate the extent to which New England clergymen had adopted a ministerial professionalism.

They similarly exaggerate the significance of the Great Awakening for this incipient professionalism. Youngs argues, for example, that ministerial professionalism was abandoned after the Great Awakening and that this had the most profound significance "for the future of American history." The creation of "a new identity" based upon the voluntary support of the people "would become an American norm" in politics as well as religion. The conceptions of clerical legitimacy and authority worked out during the 1740s were, he contends, exactly those enunciated in the 1760s and 1770s: the sovereignty of the people and the responsibility of the elite. In each case the idea that power could be legitimized by membership in an elite group was rejected "in favor of leaders who would associate with the people."[12]

Thus the argument as a whole assumes a familiar dialectical form, neatly encapsulating the presumed transit from Puritan to Yankee:

By 1750 the structure of religious leadership in colonial New England had evolved through three stages since the first Puritan settlements. In the earliest period, the ministers were admired religious leaders of a relatively harmonious society. In the second stage, the ministers sought to establish a quasi-aristocratic control over a society of contending factions. In the third stage, they based their leadership upon a principle of consent.[13]

In the final analysis, Schmotter and Youngs are able to exaggerate the data and force it into their procrustean bed of ministerial professionalism because they scrupulously limit their investigations to literary evidence, to discussions *about* power. Their footnotes and bibliographies are absolutely innocent of the actual evidence of power: church records, results of ecclesiastical councils, or, most interesting, the records of the ministerial associations themselves. If we turn our attention to the latter—to the extant recordbooks of the ministerial associations—a very different picture emerges.

Even a cursory perusal of these records reveals that while ministerial associations did indeed proliferate after the defeat of the Proposals of 1705, they did not assume any significant power over ecclesiastical affairs. Consequently, while the critics of ministerial presumption attacked the haughty attitudes of many clergymen—and even of clergymen in general—they made no mention of ministerial associations. Indeed, one searches the literature in vain for *any* reference to ministerial associations, pro or con. Finally, if the associations did not gather power to themselves, and if there was consequently no populist-inspired attack upon them, neither did the number of associations decline after the Great Awakening. Rather, they continued to proliferate, not only throughout the eighteenth century, but through the course of the nineteenth as well. It is a measure of the weakness of the professionalization argument that its proponents provide no information on the number of associations over the period they examine, though the question is central and even crucial to their argument.

The balance of this chapter will examine the distribution and exercise of ecclesiastical power during the first three quarters of the eighteenth century. Later in the book we will turn to the ministerial associations themselves in order to answer a question that may already have occurred to the reader: If ministerial associations did not accumulate and exercise power in ecclesiastical affairs, what did they do? As we shall see, they were able to play a vitally important role in ecclesiastical affairs—an integrating and cohesive role—precisely because they did *not* exercise ecclesiastical power. Lacking power, they never became the objects of struggles for power. Therein lay the secret of their success and the reason so many ministers were able to avoid the extremes of either New Lightism or Old Lightism. But this is to leap ahead of our story. The following pages, by examining the distribution of power within the ecclesiastical polity, demonstrate that the central and defining characteristic of that polity was its extreme congregationalism. The important decisions in ecclesiastical affairs were made not by ministerial associations, but by particular, virtually autonomous congregations.

II

From 1648 until 1780 Massachusetts ecclesiastical affairs were conducted along the lines laid down by the Cambridge Platform of Church Discipline. The Cambridge Platform was an ambiguous document, for while it increased the authority of ministers within their own congregations, it also guaranteed the near autonomy of the particular gathered churches and thereby limited the authority of the ministers to their individual congregations. As the preface to Chapter 15 of the platform stated, the particular churches were "distinct and therefore may not be confounded one with another; equall and therefore have not dominion over one another. . . ."[14] This near-Independency was compromised in only two ways: through the voluntary "communion of churches one with another" and through mutually chosen ecclesiastical councils. Although particular churches occasionally called upon one another for consultation, admonition, participation and other forms of "church-communion" specified in the Platform, the great bulk of ecclesiastical problems were handled by councils.

Three aspects of this council system were particularly important: (1) the councils consisted of both ministers and laymen; (2) the brethren themselves could initiate the call for a council; and (3) the councils possessed only advisory powers (in the Platform's language, they were "not to exercise church-censures in way of discipline, nor any other act of church authority, or jurisdiction. . . . "[15] Each of these provisions served as a guarantee that the ministers would not dominate the council proceedings; together they ensured that ultimate control over Massachusetts' ecclesiastical affairs would remain decentralized and under lay-control. This will become apparent if we examine each of these three provisions in turn.

Ecclesiastical councils consisted of ministers and laymen together. The usual practice was for a church whose presence had been requested at a council to send its minister and either two or three (but always more than one) laymen (called "delegates" or "messengers"). This meant that ministers were always outnumbered by laymen. It may be that the clergymen were often able to work their wills despite this disadvantage;

nevertheless, the fact remains: in any dispute between a clergyman and his congregation, the laymen could count on an ecclesiastical council dominated by laymen. Moreover, requests to attend a council were sent to the church rather than the minister, and delegates were chosen by the church.[16] It was for these reasons that ministers bent every effort to modify the council system.[17] Nothing testifies more clearly to the clergys' lack of power under the Cambridge Platform than their failure to strengthen the system of lay-dominated ecclesiastical councils.

Second, the brethren themselves could initiate the call for a council. Normally a majority of the congregation had to approve the call. The minister would then be asked to choose half of the churches to be represented, the congregation the other half. But there was nothing to prevent a minority of the congregations from calling a council of their own, and they often did. Thus, for example, when four members of the Harvard First Church found themselves dissatisfied with the Rev. John Seecomb's preaching, they wrote to several of the neighboring churches asking that they intervene.[18] Similarly, on 26 July 1757, a council of seven churches assembled at Leominster "at a request of a number of persons of ye Leominister church."[19] Or consider the events at Groveland First Church in mid-1746. At a church meeting on 11 June, the Rev. William Balch "communicated a letter dated June 9 from nine aggrieved brethren, signifying that they had invited a council to meet June 17 and asking the church's concurrence." The church refused and declared that they "will have nothing to do with said council if they come in present circumstances." But a council did convene in Groveland, the opposition of Balch and the church notwithstanding. Refused admission to the Church, they met at the home of Jonathan Hale, one of the aggrieved, conducted their hearings and filed a report with the church.[20] Their findings and recommendations were ignored, but the basic point remains: far from being dominated by the clergy, the council system provided a means whereby any aggrieved laymen, no matter how small a minority, could gain a hearing before an outside audience. Even individuals could appeal to neighboring churches for an ecclesiastical council. When, in August 1748, William Baldwin found himself at odds with his minister, he wrote for assistance to the churches at Cambridge, Newton, Weston, Medford, Scituate, Halifax, Sudbury, Reading, Worcester, Serbourn and Rutland.[21]

Third and most important, councils were advisory bodies only. As Ebenezer Parkman explained,

> They pretend to no *juridical* power, or any significance but merely what is instructive. They are nothing but some wise and good men meeting to advise ye churches how to observe ye rules most inoffensively. When they have

done all, the churches are at liberty to judge how far their advice is to be followed.[22]

This meant that a congregation dissatisfied with the results of a council simply called another, and perhaps another, until it got the decision it wanted. Thus a council that met at Bridgewater in October 1731 admonished the newly-ordained John Shaw, only to have its decision overturned by another council that sat within the same month.[23] "Councils rise against councils," Josiah Cotton complained, "and our ecclesiastical discipline is quite unhinged."[24] Sometimes ecclesiastical councils reached split decisions and filed two results, a majority report and a minority report.[25] The consequence, of course, was confusion and a heightened awareness that *no one* controlled ecclesiastical affairs in Massachusetts. When John White, minister of the church at Gloucester, published his *New England's Lamentations* in 1734 he attributed "the present weak and shattered state of our churches" largely to the prevalence of "anti-councils, whereby contrary results are given on the same case."[26]

Throughout the colonial period Massachusetts' ecclesiastical system remained an extremely decentralized polity, in which the authority that did exist was wielded by nearly autonomous congregations. In this respect, the ecclesiastical polity remained in the 1740s much as it had been in the 1640s. Hence an anonymous minister, writing during the Great Awakening, could describe Massachusetts' system of church government in almost exactly the terms used in the Cambridge Platform of 1648:

> every church and Christian society, as such, have the same right to judge and act for themselves in religious and ecclesiastical matters. And so doing, are subject to no other authority but that of Christ Jesus our lawgiver and Lord. But, while we disclaim and renounce the authority of any man, or men, over us, we, as well as our renowned ancestors before us, do not approve of the term Independent; nor are we justly chargeable with the thing, for instead of keeping at an uncomfortable distance from other churches, we steadily hold communion with them in various and considerable respects and instances.[27]

The situation in Connecticut was slightly different, for the Saybrook Platform of 1708 provided a degree of regularity and centralization over ecclesiastical affairs that was unknown in Massachusetts. However, though it compromised the autonomy of individual churches, the Saybrook Platform did not effect a substantive shift of power from laymen to clergymen, either in theory or in practice.[28] This will become apparent if we examine the key provisions of the Platform.

The movement that eventuated in the Saybrook Platform of 1708 grew out of a wide-spread feeling among Connecticut ministers and magistrates that some strengthening of church government was desirable.

This sentiment in turn sprang from the querulous state of ecclesiastical affairs in Connecticut, and out of the movement in eastern Massachusetts that had produced the Proposals of 1705. The bill originally introduced into the Connecticut General Court in May of 1708 had called for an assemblage of ministers only. But somewhere in its passage through the legislature the original wording was amended to include the crucial phrase "with such messengers [i.e., laymen] as the chhs to which they belong shall see cause to send with them."[29] The council that finally convened at Saybrook on 9 September 1708 accordingly included both ministers and laymen.[30]

The Platform that emerged from this mixed gathering did, in fact, greatly strengthen Connecticut's ecclesiastical polity. It formed the churches into county-wide "consociations," gave these bodies authority over all ecclesiastical disputes, and barred any appeal from their decisions. Churches, laymen or ministers who refused to submit to their authority would be placed under sentence of "Non-Communion" and could no longer rely upon the provincial government to force collection of their church and/or ministerial rates. These were strong measures. They abolished the near-anarchy of the council system and imbued Connecticut's ecclesiastical system with much of the procedural regularity and centralization of the English and Scottish establishments.

But did they greatly increase the power of the ministry over that of the brethren? Did the compromise of congregational autonomy mean, *ipso facto*, a compromise of lay-control as well? Most commentators believe that it did. Richard Bushman, for example, says that the Saybrook Platform gave the clergy "complete dominion" over ecclesiastical affairs in Connecticut.[31] But this is surely an exaggeration. Consider the specific provisions of the Platform. Article 2 establishes the county-wide consociations and directs that they be composed of "the particular Pastors and Chhs within the Respective Countys."[32] These were not to be clerical bodies but joint gatherings of ministers and laymen. Moreover, the Platform provided not only for the attendance of laymen, but for the probability of their numerical majority: Article 9 states that "all the Chhs of the Respective Consociations shall Choose, if they see cause, one or Two members of each Chh to represent them in the Councils. . . . "[33] Finally, steps were taken to ensure that the system of ecclesiastical ajudication created by the Platform would be as open to initiatives from below as was the council system in Massachusetts. Thus Article 7 stipulated that

> in Case any Difficultys shall arise in any of the Chhs in this Colony which cannot be Issued without Considerable Disquiet, *that Chh* in which they arise, *or that Minister, or member* aggrieved with them shall apply themselves to ye Council of

the Consociated Chhs of the Circuit to which the said Chh belongs, who if they see cause shall thereon convene, hear and determine such cases of difficulty. . . . (my emphasis)[34]

In only two instances were the clergy given powers distinct from the laity. Article 4 established the principle that ministers and lay delegates were to vote separately at consociation meetings and that the ministers had to agree to any proposal in order for it to be enacted. This article was lifted almost verbatim from Part 2, Section 6 of the Proposals of 1705. It was obviously a crucial point as far as ministerial control over ecclesiastical affairs was concerned. But, as Williston Walker has observed, the consociations actually voted by a joint ballot in which the majority of the whole formed the decision. Article 4 was, from the beginning, a dead letter.[35]

Only in Article 12 did the ministers prevail. This provision gathered the clergy of each county together in ministerial associations and charged them with "examining and Recomending the Candidates of the Ministry to the work thereof."[36] Yet even here, one is impressed less with the power given to the clergy than with the power denied them. First, the Article is not as strong as the provision in the Proposals of 1705 from which it was taken. Viewing the defeat of the earlier proposals, the Connecticut divines perhaps thought it wise to draft a milder measure. Part 1, Section 4 of the 1705 Proposals had not only given the associations authority to examine ministerial candidates, but had specifically forbidden the churches from employing any minister who had not undergone "a due Tryal by some one or other of the Associations."[37] The Saybrook Platform dropped this latter prohibition. Secondly, the ministerial associations created by the Saybrook Platform were clearly marginal concerns. The Platform's authors devoted the bulk of their attention to the consociation, and it is to them that the significant powers were assigned. Compared to the ministerial associations' ability to examine and recommend candidates for vacant pulpits, the range of powers accorded the laymen-dominated consociations were truly impressive. They included: ordination, installation and dismission of ministers; the giving of advice, direction and admonition to individual churches, ministers and laymen; the hearing of appeals from disciplinary cases tried within the individual churches; trial of clergymen accused of scandal or heresy; "and in general, deliberations and advice concerning matters of common interest to the churches."[38]

Laymen often complained about the arbitrary characteristics of their individual ministers, but one searches the literature of the eighteenth-century church disputes in vain for any complaints against ministerial associations. What one does find peppered throughout this literature is a great multitude of complaints from Connecticut ministers about the tyranny of lay-dominated consociations. In a letter to Ezra Stiles, Benjamin Gale referred to "ye Consociation, our High Court of Inquisition."[39] Similarly, John Devotion, minister of the Saybrook First Church, railed against "the undue Claims of Consociations," and warned that "Consociation Claims will make Chh.Men much faster than those Bishops" for "Lord Bishop is more palatable with many now than Lord Consociation."[40]

That the Saybrook Platform centralized and regularized the ecclesiastical system is obvious; that it gave the clergy "complete dominion" is less than obvious, for the Platform hinged not upon associations but consociations, not upon the authority of the clergy but upon the power of the brethren.

III

In this context of lay-dominated councils and consociations, the ministerial associations were absolutely powerless. This impotence sprang, first and most obviously, from the fact that both the Cambridge and Saybrook Platforms lodged effective power over ecclesiastical affairs with the brethren and ministers together, as we have seen. Ministers, as a profession and as a distinct interest group in the polity, lacked constitutional recognition and definition; therefore, they were unable to exercise power in any formal way.

The Saybrook Platform formally organized all ministers into county-wide professional associations, but the Cambridge Platform did not recognize ministerial associations at all. Lacking this constitutional recognition and impetus-to-organize, membership in Massachusetts ministerial associations remained voluntary, sporadic, haphazard and incomplete. Never were even half of the colony's clergymen organized professionally. Moreover, the associations that did exist met irregularly, did not act quickly or decisively, and characteristically dissolved after only a few years existence. Lacking real power, the associations remained evanescent, transient, feckless bodies, as liable to fade away as the early dew and the morning clouds. Jonathan Edwards' characterization of the unregenerate could as well describe the associations:

> If men do not pretend to have any oil in their vessels, what cause can there be to trust that their lamps will not go out? If they do not pretend to have any root in them, what cause is there for any disappointment when they wither away?[41]

Let us examine each of these characteristics in turn: (1) the incomplete organization of the Massachusetts clergy; (2) their usually shortlived existence; and (3) the irregularity of their meetings.

Organization of Massachusetts ministers into professional groups was haphazard, spotty and incomplete. Moreover, the evidence does not substantiate the claim that ministerial associations were expanding before the Great Awakening. Some were in decline; most continued to hold the allegiance of about half the ministers in their area. Three examples will illustrate this point: the Hampshire, Bradford and Plymouth associations.[42]

The origins of the Hampshire County Association of ministers is wrapped in obscurity. The association records do not begin until 1731.[43] In October of that year seven of the eleven ministers then settled in Hampshire County belonged to the association. During the next sixteen years their numbers rose slightly: from seven to 1731 to ten in 1740 and to eleven in 1747, when the records end. But the number of ministers settled in Hampshire County had meanwhile risen from eleven in 1731 to twenty-four in 1747. Thus the percentage of County ministers who belonged to the Association declined from 64% in 1731 to 46% in 1747. From a membership that initially included nearly two-thirds of the county's clergymen, the Hampshire Association had shrunk to less than half the county ministry when it disappeared from view. Or rather, like the churches from which it arose, its snail-like growth rate had failed to keep pace with the expansion of the population as a whole.[44]

Not all of the ministerial associations suffered such a relative decline in numbers, but none of them were able to organize the bulk of ministers in their neighborhoods. The Bradford Association, for example, was created by Thomas Symmes of Bradford in 1719 as an organization of northern Essex County ministers. For the first six years of its existence the association limped along with only seven members—less than half the ministers then residing in northern Essex County. By 1741, when the records end, the association had doubled its membership and even increased its percentage of local ministers. But it still represented only 58% of the ministers settled in that part of the colony (up from 47% in the 1719 to 1725 period).[45]

Finally, consider the history of the Plymouth Ministerial Association.[46] Created in November 1721 by Peter Thatcher of Middleborough, the Plymouth Association consisted of only six members for the first several years of its existence—less than half of the fifteen ministers settled in Plymouth County in 1721. By 1738, when it dissolved, nine members were in attendance, an increase of one-third in absolute numbers but less dramatic as an increase in percentage of all Plymouth County ministers: from 40% to 41%.

Considered simply in terms of relative numbers, there is no reason to believe that the ministerial associations experienced a significant expansion in the period before the Great Awakening. The same impression is conveyed by the relatively short life-span of most of the associations. Of those ministerial associations formed in Massachusetts before the Great Awakening, we can determine the life-span of only seven. They are:

Boston–Cambridge	1690-1704	14 years
Salem	1717-1840	123 years
Hampshire County	1731-1747	16 years
Plymouth County	1721-1738	17 years
Bradford (northern Essex County)	1719-1740	21 years
Sherburne	1702-1719	17 years
Marlborough	1725-1814	89 years

Two of these associations—the Salem and Marlborough—displayed an unusual longevity. The others lasted, on the average, only 17 years.[47]

The idea that ministerial associations were growing in numbers and strength before the Great Awakening is belied not only by their constitutional marginality, their failure to organize the bulk of Massachusetts ministers, and their generally short life span, but also by the sporadic, irregular nature of their meetings.   If attendance upon professional meetings is any indication, even those ministers who belonged to ministerial associations lacked a firm commitment to professionalism.

The experience of the Bradford Association is a case in point. At their first meeting, 3 June 1719, the founding members agreed to meet together once a month. But there is no record of their having met the following month. And at the next meeting that did occur—two months after the initial gathering—only four of the original seven ministers were present, one of them being the host. The third meeting was on 17 May 1720—nine months after the second meeting. That May 17 meeting was the only one held in 1720; 1721 and 1722 saw only one meeting each, but the Association met six times in 1723, five times in 1724, twice in 1725, and so on.[48]

One can sense, in reading through the Bradford recordbook, the disappointment and frustration that this lackadaisical attendance generated among the more serious ministers. The meeting scheduled for April 1724 was cancelled. To the next meeting on 19 May 1724, "there came only the Rev. Mr. Phillips [and] Mr. Barnard." Five members appeared for the June meeting, and they renewed their pledge to faithfully attend the monthly meetings. But no one showed up next month for the July meeting, the August meeting was cancelled by Mr. Rogers, the host, and the notation for September reads: "At Mr. Phillips—met only Mr. Barnard and Mr. Brown." At the next meeting—15 June 1725, nine months after the previous meeting—the ministers again renewed their commitment to regular attendance, in order "that the Association for the future may not be so often disappointed of coming together at our Stated times, as it has often happened in times past. . . ." And yet, at the very next meeting, the topic scheduled for discussion had to be postponed for lack of sufficient attendance. The June 1726 meeting resolved "that we endeavour to convene at the places appointed by 10 o'clock at the farthest." Yet at the next meeting the scribe noted only "Late before we came together." The July 1729 meeting, scheduled for Moses Hale's Byfield residency, had to be cancelled because "Mr. Hale forgot the meeting." In September 1729 the Association assembled at John Tuft's house in West Newbury, only to discover that Tufts was away on a journey. This haphazard pattern of attendance plagued the Association all through its existence.

The Bradford experience was typical of most ministerial associations before the Great Awakening. The Sherburne Association, for example, occasionally met every other month. But sometimes, as in 1708 and again in 1712, it failed to meet at all; and it often met only once or twice during the year.[49] If we place the number of meetings per year on a graph, it looks like this:

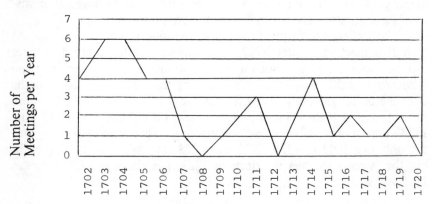

Or, again, the Plymouth Association:

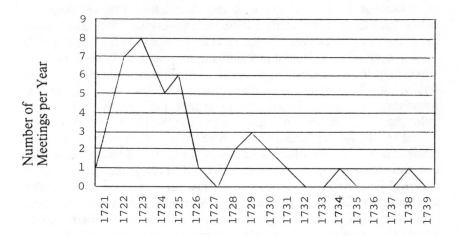

If ministerial associations were, in fact, directing the day-to-day management of ecclesiastical affairs before the Great Awakening, as the recent literature suggests, we would expect to find them convening regularly and frequently. And, if they were actually *increasing* their role in ecclesiastical affairs, we would expect to see the number of meetings increasing over time. In fact, the opposite is true: their meetings lacked any semblance of regularity, and the frequency with which they met declined rather than increased as the years went by.

Taken together, the constitutional marginality, the typically short life span, and the irregularity and declining frequency of association meetings all suggest that ministerial associations were not increasingly powerful in the period before the Awakening, but constantly powerless. They displayed the characteristics not of organizations involved in the close direction of ecclesiastical affairs, but of informal gatherings designed to provide isolated clergymen with intellectual stimulation and social camaraderie.[50]

IV

This impression of powerlessness is substantiated when we examine the actual conduct of ecclesiastical affairs. Consider first the way in which ministers were selected for vacant pulpits. Sometimes the church appeared before the local ministerial association to ask its advice. Thus, on 9 October 1733 "the people of the Place called Elbows" appeared before the Hampshire County Ministerial Association "for advice about the settlement of a minister in that place." Or again, on 10 October 1738 "The People of New-Hampton [Southampton] applied themselves to ye Association for advice, whom to apply to, to Preach to them. . . . " Or, finally, on 9 October 1745 the church at Sunderland asked the Association to suggest a candidate to assume the Rev. William Rand's pulpit, he having been recently dismissed by the church.[51]

Two things are important to note here. First, the Association offered its advice only when asked; in each case the initiative came from the church, not the Association. Second, during the sixteen years covered by the Association's records, at least twelve ministers were settled in Hampshire County. Yet only the three churches mentioned above asked the Association to suggest suitable candidates for their pulpits. Third, in not one of these three instances can it be said that the Association imposed its own candidate upon the petitioning church. In the Elbows case the Association merely ratified the church's own choice, though, as it admitted, it did so "knowing nothing concerning him, as to his doctrine, Life, or Conversation."[52] In the New Hampton case the Association acted even less decisively. At the church's first application the Association suggested "the worthy Mr. Daniel Buckingham of Milford." That advice was apparently unsatisfactory, for on 13 October 1741 the people of New Hampton again appeared before the Association and asked for the names of additional candidates. The Association accordingly supplied three more names. These too must have proved unsatisfactory, for a year later—on 12 October 1742—the New Hampton people appeared before the Association a third time and asked for yet more names. This time the Association suggested "the worthy Mr. Thomas Strong" and, in case he also failed to please, suggested that the church apply to the Boston ministers for advice.[53] In the only other case in which the Association was asked to suggest candidates for vacant pulpits—the Sunderland case—the Association declined to nominate anyone for permanent settlement.[54]

The Hampshire Association's lack of involvement in the selection of ministers by local churches epitomized the experience of other ministerial associations. For the twenty-one years of the Bradford Association's existence—from 1719 to 1740—no less than nineteen ministers were selected and settled in northern Essex County pulpits. Yet the Association was not once asked for its advice.[55] The same was true in Plymouth County. During the seventeen years that the Plymouth

Ministerial Association operated—from 1721 until 1738—thirteen pulpits were filled; yet the Association was asked to suggest candidates for only one of these.[56] It is hard to escape the conclusion that ministerial associations had little formal input into the selection of ministers by the churches in their neighborhoods. And, that what little input they did have was in the manner of advice rather than coercion. Here, as elsewhere, the laity reigned supreme.

The inability of the associations to influence (much less control) the election of ministers by the local churches was perfectly demonstrated in the struggle that erupted over Robert Breck's election to the pulpit of the Springfield First Church in 1734.[57] Breck was a liberal; as Clifford Shipton puts it, he had "quaffed a bit too thirstily at the stream of theological rationalism." The Association examined him on 8 April 1735 but declined to make any pronouncement concerning his fitness for the Springfield pulpit. It did, however, agree to mediate the dispute then raging between Breck's supporters and his critics; and for that purpose it appointed a special committee.[58]

This ad hoc committee had a distinctly conservative list, headed as it was by Jonathan Edwards and including Stephen Williams, William Williams and Nehemiah Bull, among others. Breck naturally refused to appear before it. The Liberals in his camp immediately charged that the Association was trying to usurp the right of a particular church to choose its own minister. A number of pamphlets appeared extolling the virtues of extreme congregationalism.[59] In the end the Springfield church simply chose its own ordaining council (only three of its eight members belonged to the Hampshire Association) and installed Breck on 26 July 1736.[60]

Most historians have repeated uncritically the populist-colored charges of clerical tyranny that the Breck forces leveled against the Association.[61] But the evidence does not support this interpretation; the Association was extremely reluctant to involve itself in the dispute, and in fact it never committed itself to one side or the other. Consider: the Association agreed to hear Breck on April 8 only upon his own petition (he hoped to thus publicly deny the charges of heterodoxy that had been leveled against him); after hearing him, the Association declined to offer a judgment upon his fitness for the pulpit; and it offered its further services only "if the Committee of this Association be desired to hear and Determine the matter."[62] In the end, one is struck most forcefully by the Association's obvious reluctance to get involved, and by the ease with which the Springfield church determined its own course through the entire controversy, irrespective of the Association.

What was true of the selection of ministers was also true of their ordination: ministerial associations had little to say in the matter.

William T. Youngs has recently argued that during the first four decades of the eighteenth century the clergy transformed the ordination service from a celebration of the minister's membership in a Christian fellowship to a demonstration of his separation from that fellowship and his acceptance into a more distant and distinct professional fraternity. The changes, Youngs believes, could be seen in five specifics:

> Ordination came to be performed by ministers rather than by laymen; the ordination ceremony rather than the election by the people began to be regarded as 'conveying' the ministerial office; ministers were occasionally ordained without having been chosen by the people of any particular congregation as their pastor; the ordination sermon was preached by older ministers rather than by the man being installed; and finally, in keeping with these other changes, the clergymen began to insist that the ordination day should be regarded as a solemn occasion.

Youngs believes that these changes, taken together, "indicate that the ministers now regarded themselves as a self-perpetuating body of religious leaders."[63]

Nevertheless, the larger, more pressing fact remained: it was the laity, not the clergy, that decided who would be ordained, when and where he would be ordained, and who would do the ordaining. Sometimes the ordaining council chosen by the church would consist of the local ministerial association, or some part of it. Thus, Abner Bayley was ordained over the North Metheum First Church in 1740 by John Barnard, Joseph Parsons, William Balch, Paine Wingate and Christopher Sargeant—all members of the local Bradford Association.[64] But this was unusual; more often churches chose councils composed indiscriminately of both associating and non-associating members. Of the nineteen ministers ordained in northern Essex County between 1719 and 1740—the years when the Bradford Association was sitting—only a few were ordained by Bradford Association councils.[65]

Nor did the Associations involve themselves in the dismission of ministers. William Rand's dismissal by the Sunderland First Church, for example, was not formally discussed by the Hampshire Association, though Rand had been a member of that body since its founding.[66]

Associations were more than reluctant to get involved; they regularly avoided involvement in disputes between pastors and their congregations. For example, when Benjamin Fessenden, minister of the First Church of Sandwich, fell under a cloud of popular displeasure for some moral trespass, a delegation from the church appeared before the Plymouth Association on 6 September 1725 to ask their assistance. But instead of taking on the case (Fessenden was, after all, a member of the Plymouth Association), the Association urged the unhappy brethren to call an ecclesiastical council.[67] Similarly, on 2 May 1739 the Hampshire Association received a petition from the Northfield First Church "desiring them [the Association] to use their endeavours to set them [the Northfield laity] in some suitable way which ye difficulty they labour under may be put to an end." Since Benjamin Doolittle, the Northfield minister and the subject of the petitioners' wrath, had been a member of the Hampshire Association for the past seven years, we might have expected the Association to take some measures in his defense. In fact, it suggested that the church "choose a council of other churches to come to hear, consider and determine the matter. . . . "[68] A year later, on 8 April 1740, the church again asked the Association to intervene, and again the Association refused.[69] On that same day—8 April 1740—a delegation from the New Hadley church asked the Association to look into their dispute with Grindall Rawson who had been the pastor of the New Hadley church for the past eight years. This was a serious controversy, one that would end a few months later in Rawson's removal. Moreover, Rawson had been a member of the Hampshire Association since his installation at Northfield in 1733. These might have provided motivation for the Association to act in behalf of Rawson. But instead, the Association stepped aside: "the people of New Hadley should apply to all ye churches of this county . . . as a council to hear their difficulties."[70] Association ministers would, *per force,* be a minority of such a council.

These instances are unusual only in that the local ministerial association was initially asked to intervene, or at least to render an opinion or give some advice. In most disputes the minister and his congregation simply called a mutual council, which may or may not have included association ministers. The disgruntled congregation dismissed its minister without a council in some cases (the number is small, but probably no smaller than the number of cases in which the local ministerial association was asked to intervene). For example, when Thomas Frink was refused a pay raise by his Rutland congregation, he asked to be dismissed from his pastoral relation to them. The church refused. Though a member of the Marlborough Ministerial Association, Frink did not ask that the case be referred to that body, nor did the Association formally discuss the case. The Marlborough Association was simply not involved.[71] What Frink did demand was a mutual council. As Josiah Cotton later explained, "Mr. Frink earnestly desired to be dismissed by the council, but the people having nothing to lay before them, would not come into it." Instead of calling a council, the church "dismissed him pretty roughly and abruptly."[72]

In sum, ministerial associations existed at the margins of ecclesiastical power in New England before the Great Awakening. In

Massachusetts they lacked any constitutional status, and an attempt to give them such had been defeated and was never resurrected. They never represented more than half the clergy; were not able to convene regularly or consistently, exercised no influence over the disposition of places within the profession; were unable to protect their members from the whims of their individual congregations; and usually passed into history after little more than a decade of feckless existence. The clergy as a group did not control ecclesiastical affairs in colonial New England and they knew it. But they did entertain ambitions. These ambitions and the tensions they generated are the subjects of the next chapter.

Ecclesiastical Thought
Before the Great Awakening

Sometime in the year 1718 the Rev. Peter Thatcher of Weymouth asked his congregation to dismiss him. Though he had occupied the Weymouth pulpit for over ten years, Thatcher had never been happy there. He found the weather unpleasant and the people uncongenial, and he missed his relations in Boston, where he had been born and raised. The Weymouth church initially refused his request, then refused again. Thatcher nevertheless insisted and, having grown "melancholly and indisposed in his health," was finally granted dismission by a church vote on 23 February 1718/19. No sooner had he arrived in Boston than the New North Church in that town asked him to settle with them as a colleague to the Rev. John Webb. This raised a storm of protest, for it appeared that he had left a relatively small, poor and isolated parish for a pulpit in one of Boston's largest and wealthiest churches. As Benjamin Colman explained, "We being first formed on the Congregational foot and principles, a great many of our people think the Relation between pastor and flock to be like that between husband and wife; and therefore that Mr. Thatcher has done something very hainous and foul."[1]

Except for Webb, the ministers of Boston unanimously opposed Thatcher's settlement at the New North and called an ecclesiastical council to block his ordination. But against the congregation's desire to settle Thatcher, the council's protest proved ineffectual. The New North selected an ordaining council from neighboring towns and, on 27 January 1719/20, installed Thatcher in their pulpit.

Two points about this episode deserve special consideration. First, note the freedom of action displayed by both the Weymouth and New North congregations. The Weymouth congregation, it is true, dismissed Thatcher only upon his repeated insistence. But they dismissed him themselves, without calling a council. And the New North installed him despite the explicit disapproval of the council called by the Boston ministers. Both of these actions were clear violations of the Cambridge Platform, but, as Colman observed, the Platform "is too weak a bottom, for when they will, both ministers and people will be Independent." Against the desires of a particular church, the semi-Presbyterian machinery set up by the Platform proved utterly impotent.[2]

Second, note the similar impotence displayed by the Boston ministers. Here was a case in which the town's ministry stood virtually united — but to no purpose. Neither the system of ecclesiastical councils, nor the mobilized opposition of all the local ministers (one only excepted) could prevent the brethren of the New North from working their will. In Massachusetts church affairs, as this single example suggests and as the previous chapter demonstrated, the laity reigned supreme.

Moreover, the incident sheds an interesting light upon clerical attitudes toward ecclesiastical authority before the Great Awakening, which is the subject of the present chapter. In Benjamin Colman's relation of the episode, contained in a letter he sent to the Rev. Robert Wodrow in Scotland, Colman implied that the clergy had not objected to Thatcher's settlement as vigorously as they might have. At one point he wrote, "all this disorder is owing to the want of Presbyterian Authority and Jurisdiction among us." But then, a few lines further on, he added that this constitutional defect operated "together with our cowardly Silence and only Silent testimony against it" to "run us into all these Confusions."[3]

One can sympathize with the clergy's "cowardly Silence," for the episode presented them with the necessity of choosing between two primary values, suddenly thrown into conflict. On the one hand, they opposed Thatcher's installation for moral and constitutional reasons. Morally, his apparent desertion of rural Weymouth for a large, prestigious pulpit in the metropolis seemed, as Coleman put it, "something very hainous and foul" — something akin to the breaking of a marriage covenant. In opposing his installation, the Boston ministers imagined themselves standing up for the welfare of rural congregations against the self-interest of ambitious and unscrupulous clergymen. Moreover, the constitutional issue loomed large in their minds. What would be the consequences for ecclesiastical order if churches could dismiss and/or ordain ministers, not only without leave of ecclesiastical councils, but in direct opposition to their decisions? Colman was probably not the only man who sat down at his desk "to think of these Motions, whither they tend."[4]

On the other hand, if the ministers acted to block Thatcher's installation (as they did, though apparently without the resolution Colman thought necessary), they could be charged with attempting to subvert the right of a particular church to choose its own minister. Which is exactly what happened: the Thatcher group based their case squarely on the rock of congregational autonomy and accused the opposition of attempting to impose a coercive Presbyterianism on Massachusetts churches.[5]

The clergy's ambivalence is thus understandable. And that ambivalence provides a key insight into the way they thought about ecclesiastical affairs before the Awakening. For throughout the Colonial period, the clergy found itself torn between its growing desire for ecclesiastical order, system, and regularity on the one hand, and on the other its commitment to congregational principles. The ministers' emerging professionalism (described below) gave them a vivid sense of the need for reform. At the same time, their will to act was inhibited by their commitment to Congregationalism and their knowledge that the laity in fact controlled ecclesiastical affairs and was demonstrably hostile to schemes for reform. Their commitment to constitutional order impelled them to block Thatcher's installation, but their commitment to congregationalism (whether out of principle or from a fear of antagonizing the laity) made their action hesitant, "cowardly" and, in the end, ineffectual.

The pages that follow discuss this ambivalence by examining the sense of professionalism articulated by some clergymen in the first four decades of the eighteenth century, and the attempt by other ministers to limit the claims of professionalism when they seemed to threaten the prerogatives of the laity or the principle of congregational semi-autonomy as enunciated by the Cambridge Platform.

I

During the first four decades of the eighteenth century many New England clergymen came to think of themselves as a distinct fraternity of professionals, abstracted from the mundane affairs of daily life.[6]

The core of this "clerical professionalism" lay in its conception of the ministry as a distinct fraternity. Thus the frequent clerical reference to ordination as a "solemn separation to the work of the ministry." Ministers "must needs be very faulty if they needlessly incumber themselves with worldly affairs," explained William Shurtleff of Portsmouth. And, conversely, "the people must needs be very criminal, that tempt or oblige them to it." John Hancock of Lexington cautioned laymen not to place their ministers "under a necessity of labouring in the field." And John Tufts of the Newbury Second Church warned that "when they are obliged to . . . employ themselves in as mean and despicable [a] business as their ordinary neighbors, it makes unthinking people, who judge according to outward appearance, to look upon themselves as good and great and wise as their ministers . . ." Toiling in the fields tended to "darken their minds." Rather than working the earth, ministers were set aside to cultivate their minds, to become, in Tufts' words, "universal scholars." Other ministers concurred. Thomas Clap of Windham, Connecticut, thought ministers should furnish themselves with good libraries and "have no worldly cares and pressures, that may hinder their reading of them, and diligent prosecution of their studies."[7]

This close association of ministerial duties with intellectual labor reveals the clergy's growing conviction that their profession was defined not by the spiritual state of its members as much as by their possession of a special technical knowledge. Ministerial candidates had to master not only Greek, Latin and Hebrew, but "the whole circle of Arts and Sciences." This sort of knowledge, as the clergy was fond of pointing out, could only be acquired with much labor and study—study that exhausted the flesh, wearied the spirit and consumed time. The Apostles may have been qualified for their ministerial labors by the convenient and less arduous method of spiritual inspiration, but such qualifications were no longer sufficient.

> Ministers of Christ now should in the ordinary way of diligent labor, study and prayer, be accomplished, as far as may be, with those gifts of tongues and knowledge which were [once] given to them in an extraordinary manner.

Those who expected to receive divine guidance in their preparation for the ministry were, in Charles Chauncy's estimation, "miserably deluded." Ministers had to possess "the best advantages of learning and education to accomplish them for their difficult work."[8]

Along with this perception of themselves as a profession, complete with its own technical language, specialized knowledge and lengthy, time-consuming preparation, went an increasing preoccupation with ordering and codifying that knowledge and with establishing regular procedures for its employment. Thomas Clap advised prospective candidates for the ministry to

> read the Word of God with this particular view: to draw rational inferences and deductions from it, [and] to consult what authors have wrote upon what subject.

Clergymen familiar with British and European Reformed churches were often distressed and dismayed at the pragmatic, disorganized approach to ecclesiastical procedure that seemed to prevail in New England church affairs. Clap complained that "we have few or no stated and known rules for a minister's direction, as there is in the Church of Scotland, and some other well-reformed Churches." New Englanders seemed to act "only *pro hic et nunc*, as suited the occasion":

> When any case comes upon the Board, the rule seems to be, not to do what is just and right in itself, but what may happen to serve the present turn . . . hence one ecclesiastical judgment is no precedent for another, and same methods are not always observed in same cases, but things left fluctuating in uncertainties.

Clap thought the absence of regular procedures a central cause of the "distempered Heats" that continually rocked colonial churches. It gave parishioners, he thought, "occasion of quarrelling with one another, involved their ministers in difficulties, and exposed them to the odious aspersions and imputations of partiality, unsteadiness and the like." Clap thought the problem could be solved by commissioning "some aged and experienced New England Divine" to collect the rules and procedures used in Reformed churches in Scotland and France and make them available to the New England clergy.[9]

As ministers became increasingly conscious of their role as a distinct, highly professionalized fraternity, they also began to evince a concern with entrance into the profession. "To admit unqualified persons," Clap warned, "has a tendency to . . . bring scandel upon religion." Nathaniel Henchman of Lynn thought that the clergy had a duty to "maintain the honour of their ministry" by admitting only those who possessed the requisite professional credentials. "Lay hands suddenly on no man," he advised, for "introducing persons unqualified into the ministry" would only produce "ill consequences" and "give occasion that the ministry be blamed."[10]

All of these developments — the difference between the lives of ministers and laymen, the entrance into a distinct fraternity, the sense of professional attitudes and competence — were graphically symbolized in the manner of ordination that became common in the early decades of the eighteenth century. During the seventeenth century the ordination had been performed by laymen, signifying, in J.W.T. Youngs' judgment, "the minister's position as a member and leader of a fellowship of Christian believers." But during the first three decades of the eighteenth century the New England ministers began ordaining one another, symbolically obviating the need for public justification. The climax of these increasingly elaborate ceremonies came when the presiding minister gave "the Right Hand of Fellowship" to the initiate, signifying his acceptance into a special fraternity. Rather than celebrating "the minister's position as a member and leader of a fellowship of Christian believers," the ordination ceremony had come to symbolize his separation from that community and elevation above it. As Thomas Clap explained, the ordination service "raised [ministers] above the cares and necessities of humane life."[11]

In these and other ways, many clergymen displayed their conviction that clerical authority was institutional, rather than personal or charismatic, that ecclesiastical power flowed from organization, regularized procedures, and specialized knowledge. The thrust of many clergymen's thinking was in the direction of effecting a radical disjuncture of personal character and ecclesiastical power. The New England churches were to be presided over by priests rather than prophets. It is "by our office," William Shurtleff of Portsmouth reminded his colleagues, "that we are as it were raised up. . . ." When Thomas Clap of Windham, Connecticut officiated at the ordination of Ephraim Little over the First Church of Colcester, he told Little's new congregation to receive him not "as a man by nature," but "as an angel by office." In a 1733 sermon entitled *The Divine Pastor*, Nathaniel Henchman of Lynn explained that the efficacy of the sacraments depended not upon the personal holiness of the clergyman that administered them, but upon the divine origin of his office, upon his "godly warrent." Ministers may be "small and inconsiderable in Appearance," but by the "dignity of the sacred function" and "the extensive greatness of their office," they were "rais'd above the common level and plac'd in a superior rank among men." As another minister observed, "the pastoral office magnifies the minister. . . ." Even were a particular clergyman to display the marks of a corrupt heart, "this does not vacate his commission, nor make it that he had no commission."[12]

Many clergymen justified this disjuncture of personal sanctity and ecclesiastical power by reference to a basic tenet of Calvinist orthodoxy: the elusive quality of divine election, the fact that the condition of one's soul was largely hidden from public inspection and examination. "These things have all their existence in the soul," explained Jonathan Edwards, "which is out of our neighbors' view." Similarly Edwards' archantagonist, Charles Chauncy of Boston's First Church: "Can it be supposed," Chauncy asked, "that sanctifying grace should be necessary to a regular or valid administration of Gospel-Ordinances, when 'tis the sole prerogative of the great God to know the persons that are endowed with it?" If the sacraments were effective only when administered by a sanctified heart, how were communicants to know whose administration to attend upon?

> For all [and] anything we know, or indeed can know . . . the ministers we most admire, and have the highest opinion of, as eminently santified men, may be no

> other than whited sepulchres, beautiful without, but within, full of dead men's bones, and all rottness and uncleanness.[13]

Confining the success of Gospel ordinances to the inward sanctity of the ministers seemed not only unreasonable and impracticable, but "unchristian" as well.

> The grace which is exhibited in or by the Sacraments, rightly used, is not conferred by any power in them [i.e., the ministers]; neither doth the efficacy of a sacrament depend upon the piety, or intention of him that doth administer it; but upon the work of the spirit, and the word of the institution.[14]

Thus many ministers, in the early decades of the eighteenth century, effected a radical disjuncture of personal sanctity and ecclesiatical power. Ministerial authority rested not upon the holiness of the clergy but upon regularized church procedures and the professional training and competence of the ministry. It was, as Edward Holyoke, the president of Harvard College, explained, "according to the importance of their posts" that laymen were to "give them reverence and esteem, and submit to the authoritative sentence as it is by them pronounc'd . . ."[15]

This interpretation of their authority as institutional rather than personal gave the ministers, according to some of them, an almost unrestricted hand in governing their churches. As Ebenezer Parkman of Westborough explained, "the Gospel alloweth no church authority (or rule properly so called) to the brethren but reserveth that wholly to ye elders." Ministers, according to Parkman, "are to prepare beforehand [and] withall declare to ye church ye counsel and will of God therein — he proceedeth whether ye people obey it or no." Although the laity had "a power belonging unto them," this was a power "which they should exercise in their place," that is, "not in opposition to their pastor . . . but for the incouraging his heart, and strengthening his hands, that he may order and regulate the affairs of Christ's kingdom."[16]

This greatly expanded conception of clerical authority was articulated over and over again in the early decades of the eighteenth century. "Obey them which have the rule over you," Nathaniel Eells of Norwell commanded, "and submit yourselves to their godly instruction and discipline." Ministers "are set as overseers of their people," William Williams of Hatfield contended. "The teaching and ruling authority in the churches, Christ hath joined together." As John Tufts of Newbury put it, "Jesus Christ has committed unto them the keys of the kingdom of heaven, and made them rulers over his household." Ecclesiastical order required that ministers possess "the advantage of a sufficient degree of power to execute the will of God." They must not be "so dependent upon the wills or humors of men, as to be under any discouraging fears of doing their duty." Nathaniel Henchman referred to ministers as "rulers in (God's) house" and insisted that they ruled according to Scripture, as interpreted by themselves alone.

> Nor may it be authoritatively demanded of Christ's ministers to subscribe to . . . any humane scheme, form, or model of government in the church, but such as is plainly declared in, or by necessary consequences may be deduced from the Scriptures.

When John Devotion of Saybrook was confronted with a demand from one of his parishioners for more frequent church meetings, he responded, as he later told Ezra Stiles of Newport, by "letting him know that when the office of the ministry could not be executed without menace, it was time to think seriously of consequences."[17]

Thus, by the fourth decade of the eighteenth century many New England clergymen had developed an expanded and exaggerated conception of their own role. To large numbers of ministers it seemed that not only ecclesiastical order, but the very success of the original "errand into the wilderness" had come to rest upon their shoulders alone. In a passage strikingly reminiscent of John Winthrop's "Christian Charity," Eliphat Adams of New London revealed the extent to which some clergymen had abrogated unto themselves the mission originally meant to inspire the entire community. "We are," Adams wrote of the clergy in 1730,

> as a city set upon a hill, all people's eyes are upon us to make their observations. If we miscarry in our conduct, if we preach unsound doctrine, if we vary from the just rules of our holy discipline, or if we prove but mean examples of living, there will be enough to spy it out, who will be forward to expose and condemn us, and what is worse, our consciences will reproach us, and our blessed Lord and master will never own us in this.[18]

Adams was not the only minister to use such pregnant imagery. In 1727 William Shurtleff urged his colleagues to "remember that they are in a peculiar manner the Lights of the World; that they are as a City set upon a Hill, which cannot be hid." And only the year before Thomas Foxcroft had declared that ministers occupied an "elevated and conspicuous station, [for] they are as a City set on a Hill, which can't be hid."[19]

II

Much of the literature on the ministry in the eighteenth century focuses upon the clergy's attempt to expand their authority. The reasons for this are not difficult to find. First, many ministers *were* presumptuous and *did* claim an exaggerated authority over their parishioners, as we have seen. But second, and more importantly, the depiction of a tyrannical ministry attempting to force the yoke of clerical dominion upon their freedom-loving congregations allows the historian to work within a familiar and fashionable Neo-Progressive interpretive framework. In the studies by Schmotter, Youngs and others, the story of ecclesiastical politics in the first half of the eighteenth century assumes a shape that anyone familiar with the works of Carl Becker, Charles Beard or Arthur Schlesinger will recognize immediately: a domineering elite attempts to extend its quasi-aristocratic control over society; for reasons of its own — in this case to stimulate flagging church membership — the elite is forced to mobilize the populace; but through this partially-opened door rush forces that the elite cannot control; in the end the elite is overwhelmed, the popular party emerges victorious, and the polity is restructured to accommodate their demand for inclusion and participation.[20]

The difficulties with this interpretation are three-fold. First, as we will see below, the clergy were nowhere as united as this interpretation asserts. Many ministers did seek to expand clerical authority, but just as many thought such attempts unwise and unprincipled and spoke out against them. Second, though the Great Awakening did unleash a torrent of criticism against individual ministers, it did not generate any sustained assault upon either the ecclesiastical polity or upon the ministry as a group. Third, most ministers welcomed the Awakening (though guardedly), tried to take advantage of the religious interest it generated, and, when it had passed, expressed deep and genuine disappointment.

Clerical response to the Awakening will be examined in the next chapter. The remainder of this chapter will attempt to balance the picture of clerical professionalism sketched above by describing the criticism that this emerging professionalism generated within the clergy.

The exaggerated claims of clerical authority expressed by many clergymen in the first four decades of the eighteenth century, described above, were not descriptions of ecclesiastical reality but reactions to ecclesiastical impotency. As we saw in Chapter 1, ecclesiastical decisions, in both theory and practice, were largely controlled by the laity. "In the Congregational Way," as Samuel Mather of the Boston Second Church explained in 1738, "the Empire of the Clergy is further forsaken than in any other form of church government."[21]

Moreover, the clergy as a class received neither the respect nor the deference and submission that many of them thought their just due — as they themselves admitted repeatedly. "I am sensible," William Shurtleff of Portsmouth admitted in 1739, "that the ministers of Christ are thought altogether unnecessary, and instead of blessings, are esteemed as unprofitable burdens by some of the world." Nathaniel Henchman of Lynn thought that the ministry had "fallen into the dregs of time," that clergymen were "meanly accounted of and with supercilious grandeur disparaged." William Rand of Sunderland complained that "persons who are carnel and sensual, who mind earthly things, will not readily see and acknowledge that the ministerial function is desirable and honourable." Eliphat Adams of New London reported that "many will scarce give us the hearing; they lurk at home perhaps all the year around . . . and if we go after them into the mountains and thickets, we can scarce find them out, or obtain any favourable audience, or meet with a cordial welcome." Even when they did come to church, many laymen seemed to be "ever carping at the doctrine or bespattering the names or weakening the hands or grieving the hearts of their faithful ministers." It seemed to Adams, and to other New England clergymen, that "there is but little good done by their preaching"; they were listened to by none but "a few sick and dying people, who now, perhaps, at last want to know what they shall do to be saved."[22]

Some ministers attributed this disparagement to the clergy's attempt to discipline their people. Samuel Niles of Kingston thought that laymen "think themselves unreasonably restrained" by church discipline. As Joseph Baxter of Mendon explained, "ministers must many times necessarily doe those things which sinners are displeased with and enraged at." Grindall Rawson wrote that ministers suffered because "the true Christian religion does not allow persons that liberty and elbow-room to enjoy their lusts and their corruptions as the Mahometan religion does."[23]

But other ministers were able to see that the clergy often brought this ridicule upon themselves by their demands for deference and their attempts to extend their dominion over their parishioners. After describing the contempt many laymen displayed toward their ministers, Edward Holyoke, president of Harvard College, admitted that "the pride of some of the Order in the world, aspiring after rule and dominion, hath very much provok'd this treatment," that they had "too much exalted their state and the dignity of their office." In 1724 Samuel Stoddard of Northampton warned his colleagues that "the multiplying of ceremonies" made laymen contemptuous of clerical authority. In 1738 Samuel Mather contended that if parishioners refused to respect their ministers, it was because so many clergymen "seem to be fond of one minister's ruling and governing his own church without the consent of the brethren. . . ." "Can [the laity] be easy," John White of Gloucester asked in 1734, "when those who by divine appointment are to minister to them for their spiritual edification, lord it over them? . . . Will Englishmen tamely submit thereto?"

> There are many dark clouds hung over New-England, and the churches of Christ therein, but I apprehend this to be as dark and dismal as any. To go from the Rule [of the Cambridge Platform] is Arbitrary; and to go against professed principles, making [ministers'] wills the rule, is tyranny. And when people fairly possessed of liberties and priviledges, are thus dealth with this leads directly to contention and confusion.[24]

Because they recognized that clerical presumption and conceit often antagonized the laity, and because they recognized their close dependence upon the laity, these ministers advised their colleagues to adopt a more modest and humble conception of themselves and their profession.   John Hancock of Lexington urged his fellow ministers to display "more wisdom and more grace, than to make so much trouble about secular honor and promotion."   It would be to their own advantage, he explained, "to be more humble, and to watch against ambition," for "temporal power and jurisdiction belongs to the princes of the gentiles, and not unto the ministers of Christ."   Thomas Foxcroft of the Boston First Church charged that the claims to deference and respect raised by some of his colleagues "seems to me carry'd up to a greater height considerably than is either usually practised by elders, or in fact allowed by the brethren."   Rather than continuing to   press their demands, he thought it would "behoove them as ministers, to deny themselves, to deny their own opinions and wills and rights. . . ."   In 1738 Samuel Mather warned the clergy that their hunger for ecclesiastical power might very well be insatiable and, for that reason, might carry them into paths that would utterly destroy congregationalism. "From a congregation and clasis, you must go to a provincial synod. And where next? To a national synod. And what will you do then? Afterwards you must go to a general ecumenical council."   Benjamin Colman of the Brattle Street Church in Boston similarly warned his colleagues of the dangers of ministerial pride.   "We did not become ministers," he reminded them, "because we were better born, nor because we were sons of brighter parts, nor because we had better hearts than others . . . How many of us may rather say . . . 'I was no prophets son, but a tradesmans'?"   Ministers, he reminded them, "are given *for the people* and *to* the people; not *they* formed into congregations and churches for the sake of ministers."[25]

These clergymen denied the generalized demands for respect and authority voiced by some of their colleagues; and they advised them to moderate their claims and adopt a more humble and submissive attitude toward their parishioners. But this is not all: they also countered many of their colleagues' more extravagant demands, one by one; and in doing so they reaffirmed the Congregational ideal of a "middle way" between the demands of the clergy and the rights of the laity.

One of the issues thus debated concerned the question of whether a minister's authority extended beyond the bounds of his own parish. In the 1720s and 1730s some clergymen, when ordaining younger men into the ministry, pretended to give them an authority to administer the sacraments in churches other than their own. For example, when Samuel Phillips of the Andover South Church ordained Timothy Walker in November of 1730, he told Walker that "power is given to you to perform *all ministerial acts*, not only in this place, but in *other* places also . . ." (emphasis in the original). Moreover, some ministers explicitly defended this doctrine and practice. In 1734, for example, Nathaniel Eells of Norwell contended that ordination in one church gave a minister authority in "the Church of God in general," that "although he presides over one flock, yet his power to preach and administer the sacraments reacheth to other places and other people." Eells later withdrew this argument, but his original contention, and the practice it defended, raised a storm of protest within the clergy. In 1730 Nathaniel Mather's *A Discussion of the Lawfulness of a Pastor's Acting as an Officer in Other Churches*, originally published in the 1680s, was reprinted in Boston as a protest against "the irregular practice of some church or churches who called neighboring pastors in to administer the Lord's Supper to them when they had none of their own [and] such like practices here of late." This practice was particularly objectionable, according to the eighteenth century preface, because it extended the authority of ministers "beyond the bounds which Christ hath set by making it reach to *OFFICE POWER*." Ministers had "thereby fallen into a mistake which is in itself destructive to the nature of a spiritual corporation." For "if ministerial power be communicable . . . what becomes of particular churches and their privileges?" The autonomy of individual churches could not survive unless ministers reaffirmed the principle that each pastor "belongs to his church and to no other." These sentiments were seconded by other clergymen. John Tufts of Newbury insisted that membership in a particular church was as important as ordination itself in qualifying one to administer the sacraments; no one could serve communion who was not both member and minister. And John White made the same point in *New England's Lamentations*. In his *Apology for the Liberties of the Churches in New England,* Samuel Mather argued that even the Apostles had not indulged in "at-large" ordinations and contended that excepting "only some Ecclesiastical Don Quixotes" the New England clergy generally "judge it an absurd and extravagant thing."[26]

The election of ministers by particular churches was another area in which some clergymen tried to expand clerical authority. And here too they were met by criticism from their colleagues. For example, shortly before his death in 1725, the Reverend Thomas Symmes of Bradford wrote a paper for his congregation entitled "Advice and instructions about choosing a minister" to succeed him. In these instructions he told his parishioners that "ordinarily the neighboring ministers are most proper judges, who is most suitable for their neighborhood." In choosing his successor, he told them, "don't needlessly and unreasonably act without it, much less divers from it, or contrary to it," for "this is disorderly and unneighborly, and of a very fatal tendency." Similarly, Ebenezer Parkman of Westborough thought that although

> a church has a right to choose their own pastor, nevertheless, a church in ye exercise of that right ought in all possible ways consistent . . . to consult ye edification and satisfaction of ye neighbors . . . churches may suffer their elections to be *directed*, yea to be *diverted* by considerations which they owe to others in ye vicinity without surrendering their liberty . . . (emphasis in original).[27]

In fact, as we saw in Chapter 1, laymen did not ordinarily consult with the neighboring clergy — or at least not formally with the neighboring associations of ministers. This seemed to many clergymen an altogether satisfactory arrangement. Benjamin Colman reported in 1717 that "our good people chuse their own pastors" and that "they chuse well ordinarily . . ." Others urged the laity to defend their right of election, and criticized clerical attempts to infringe, abridge or restrict that right. "Tis the right and priviledge of the Brethren to chuse their offices," John White contended; "they should not be discouraged or obstructed in the use of their just liberties." John Hancock defended the formula of *"election* by the people and *ordination* at the hands of the presbytery," and wrote that the laity "ought not to slight and priviledge, or needlessly surrender it unto others, but they should stand fast in the liberty which Christ and the Christian magistrate has put into their hands." Samuel Mather argued that men should enjoy the same liberty in religious affairs that they exercise in civil life: "Men can chuse their friends, their lawyers, their physicians; and can there be any good reason assigned, why they should be hindered from the exercise of the like liberty in spiritual regards? Truely no!" He then went on to address directly the arguments of those clergymen who wanted to limit and compromise lay choice of ministers:

> If it should be granted, that the people may grow factious and troublesome in their elections, and confusions should arise by means of them, what then? All that this proves is that churches may degenerate, and who denies that? But such degeneracy in them is to be lamented and reformed: and the people should still possess and enjoy their priviledge of chusing their officers . . . the objections against their enjoyment of this liberty are of no force and validity.[28]

Or consider the question of Ruling Elders. Chapter four of the Cambridge Platform had authorized Ruling Elders in order to establish a source of power that would stand midway between an individual clergyman and his congregation. As an anonymous layman explained in 1731, the office was intended both to "shelter [the minister] from suspicions of acting arbitrarily . . . *and* [to] prevent him from doing so." Thomas Foxcroft elaborated upon this argument in the same year. To allow ministers to handle church discipline alone was thought by many "as unavoidably inferring too great a diversion from [the pastors'] proper employ . . . and exposing them to the censures of envious, discontented people. . . ." The office of Ruling Elder established "a mixt administration (which cannot be where there is not a plurality of elders)."[29]

However, during the seventeenth century the office gradually fell into disuse. As early as 1650 only one-third of the New England churches employed a plurality of elders. By 1724, as Joseph Sewall of the Old South Church in Boston reported, "there is but one elder [i.e., the minister] in by far the greatest part of them." This meant that in cases of church discipline the ministers, according to Benjamin Colman, "act more their own will and pleasure than if they had a Presbytery or consistory of elders. . . ."[30]

In those few churches where ruling elders were instituted, they performed a wide range of important functions. For example, on 9 October 1730 the First Church of Groveland chose five men to serve as ruling elders and specified their functions as follows:

> 1st, in watching over the manners of the brethren. 2nd, in examining reports and stories to the prejudice of one or another. 3rd, in dealing with offenders, ripening and preparing matters for the church being of a public nature, and [4th], making up in private such things as will admit of a private healing.[31]

That the ruling elders did, in fact, join with the pastor (William Balch) in "ripening" cases of church discipline for presentation to the church is apparent from the next entry in the church records:

At a church meeting Deborah, ye wife of James Wallingford, was convicted by sufficient evidence of ye sin of hard and excessive drinking, and it was voted that the brethren of the church do concur with the elders in suspending of her from communion . . .[32]

Because ruling elders did play a significant role in church affairs, many ministers regarded the office as an infringement of their authority and resisted its establishment. When the parishioners of John Hancock's Lexington Church asked him to install two ruling elders he responded affirmatively and told his congregation that he had studied the question in some depth and knew exactly what the new officers should do:

I should like to have one of them come up to my house before meeting on Sunday and get my horse out of the barn, and then saddle him and bring him up to the door, and hold the stirrup while I get on. The other may wait at the church door and hold him while I get off; then, after meeting, he may bring him up to the steps. This is all of my work I ever can consent to let the ruling elders do for me.

At this point the matter was dropped and the Lexington church went on without ruling elders.[33]

When the First Church at Milford called Amariah Frost to their pulpit they stipulated that he must select two ruling elders to assist him with matters of church discipline. Frost "meekly agreed," but a minority of the ordaining ministers balked. The majority went ahead with the ordination, but the incident is suggestive of clerical attitudes toward ruling elders.[34]

Nevertheless, a significant number of clergymen defended the brethren's right to elect ruling elders, and even encouraged them to do so. "Are these churches sufficiently furnished with officers to attend to weighty services of feeding, ruling and watching over the flocks?" asked Joseph Sewall. "Are there not some cases in which it will be very difficult if not impracticable for the church to act according to our constitution, as when the pastor is personally engaged with any of the brethren?" Samuel Mather declared that the office of ruling elders had been an integral part of the Apostolic churches, and that for any to deny the office "must reflect upon the holy Apostles, and even upon the wisdom of our great Savior." John White similarly defended "the right and priviledge of the brethren to chuse their officers," and argued that "if the reverend pastors will be so arbitrary as utterly to refuse to call the church together to chuse these officers, I suppose the church may look upon themselves, in that case, and so far, to be without a ruler, and may convene for this purpose, as when they have no minister."[35]

The office of ruling elders seemed to many the key to a "middle way" between clerical tyranny and lay anarchy. As an anonymous writer put it in 1731: "If any can give an instance of any churches in the world who have slighted that order of men, and have not turned into *Anarchy* or *Prelacy* within less than one century, I should be glad to have it produced." No one stated this ideal more clearly than the Rev. Edward Goddard of Framingham in June of 1739. "I have heard a good deal of talk about the power of ministers and the duty of the people to obey them," he confided in his commonplace book.

> Some of the talk seemed to me to have a tendency to ecclesiastical tyranny and slavery, and some of it to introduce anarchy or popularity. I could not persuade myself to submit to the former, nor fall in with the latter, nor could I find out a medium till after much debate in my mind. I happened to fix upon the following opinion about the rule or authority which Christ hath insituted in his church, viz, . . . the scriptures plainly intimate a plurality of elders in every church . . . I cannot find 1 instance in Scripture of a church placed under the government of one single pastor or ruler, nor any charge given to any minister to undertake such an office as that of a sole ruler of a church . . . appointing a number of elders to preside in ecclesiastical matters . . . is adapted to promote an impartial administration of ecclesiastical and judicatures and is supported not only by the highest human reason, but also by the whole current of the Scripture.[36]

Consider, finally, the problem of congregational autonomy. Clerical writings of the eighteenth century are peppered with complaints about what the clergy regarded as the near-anarchy of New England's ecclesiastical polity. Nor were these denunciations confined to Massachusetts clergymen: even some of those living under the Saybrook Platform found it a weak and ineffective instrument. Eleazar Wheelock of Lebanon, Connecticut, for example, complained repeatedly of "ye feeble and languishing state of church government" in that province. "After all we can do," he wrote in 1739, "it is very lame." After reviewing a book on the organization of church affairs in Scotland, Benjamin Colman wrote, "I wish heartily that we were here under any like authoritative regimen." Many New England clergymen were afraid of the "Popish" sentiments of some of their colleagues, he admitted, but "I am much more afraid of the Antinomian Lisp among the brethren." Josiah Cotton of Plymouth condemned "ye dangerous circumstances of our ecclesiastical constitution, for want of a decisive power. . . ." Throughout the century, both before and after the Awakening, clergymen sought to limit and restrict the near-autonomy of the particular churches.[37]

Yet at least as many ministers defended the autonomy and authority of the congregations. "Let councils move in their proper sphere," advised John White in 1734; "let them give advice and hold forth light, do that and proceed no farther." Similarly, Ebenezer

Parkman thought that councils, synods and ministerial associations should "pretend to no *juridical* power," that after they had offered their thought on a particular case, "the churches are at liberty to judge how far their advice is to be followed." He believed that "it will be most safe to preserve to ye church of brethren their due liberty." Perhaps the most vigorous and outspoken champion of congregational automony was Samuel Mather of the Boston Second Church. "There may be synods or meetings of pastors for promoting peace and concord," he admitted in 1734; "but there is great danger, lest such meetings should be hurtful to the principles and liberties of particular churches . . . If we once depart from a particular church for jurisdiction, we shall be wise beyond what is written and run wild in our imagination."[38]

Thus we can see that on the eve of the Great Awakening, New England clergy had not altogether abandoned Congregationalism in favor of the new professionalism. Rather, the claims of ministerial authority and ecclesiastical centralization were met by a reaffirmation of the rights of the laity and the independence of the particular gathered churches. The existence and strength of this reaffirmation—which was, after all, only a reaffirmation of New England's Middle Way—would help some clergymen chart a moderate course through the turmoil of the Great Awakening.

The Clergy and the Great Awakening

"We see so many persons in common life *halting, wavering* and *vibrating* between different opinions, with . . . such a compound of opposite *qualities, humours* and *inclinations,* that we are, all our lives long, at a loss to determine with precision, what is such a man's predominant and ruling principle of action."

Egerton Leigh, *The Man Unmasked: Or, The World Undeceived* . . . (Charleston, 1769), as quoted by Michael Kammen, *People of Paradox* (1972)

The character of those men who sought the "middle-way" is particularly important to an understanding of the process that shaped the "Old Calvinist" party. It was this cluster of New England clergymen who reformulated the assumptions of Calvinism in a manner particularly suited to the exigencies of religious life in the middle of the eighteenth century. None of the Old Calvinist leaders participated in the revivals of the Great Awakening; indeed, some of them criticized what they believed were the excesses of the revivalists. But they were not overtly hostile or critical of the Awakening as a whole and none of the old Calvinists participated in the various attempts to squash the revivals. Conversely, though some of the revivals' most out-spoken critics eventually identified with Old Calvinism, none of them played a leading or influential role in that movement.

There was, then, a particular temperament that distinguished the leading Old Calvinists from the evangelical Calvinists on their left and from the Arminian Calvinists on their right. The following chapter briefly describes the role played by New Light preachers in the Awakening, then contrasts this with the response of the Old Lights, focusing especially upon the response of Charles Chauncy, the acknowledged leader of the New England Old Lights. The final section describes the way in which certain moderate-minded Calvinists responded to the Awakening. It was out of this final group that the Old Calvinist party emerged in the late 1750s and early 1760s.

I

During the 1730s various and scattered congregations had experienced spiritual revivals. But it was not until the English evangelist George Whitefield toured the colonies in 1739 that the Great Awakening really took on the dimensions of a mass social movement. Whitefield's powerful preaching ignited the spiritual sensibilities of thousands and his influence reached into virtually every congregation in the northern and middle colonies.

News of Whitefield's approach drew men and women from their work for miles in every direction. We have a remarkable description of the excitement that preceded Whitefield's journey through Connecticut written by a Kensington farmer named Nathan Cole. Cole had heard of Whitefield preaching "like one of the old Apostles" in Philadelphia, and had followed the reports of his progress through New York and New Jersey. Early one morning, while working in his field, Cole heard that Whitefield was coming to nearby Middletown, that he was to preach that very morning. Cole's report of what followed is worth repeating in its entirety for he vividly captured the sense of excitement and anticipation that Whitefield generated everywhere he went.

> I dropt my tool that I had in my hand and ran home to my wife telling her to make ready quickly to go and hear Mr Whitefield preach at Middletown, then run to my pasture for my horse with all my might; fearing that I should be too late; having my horse I with my wife soon mounted the horse and went forward as fast as I thought the horse could bear, and when my horse got *much* out of breath I would get down and put my wife on the Saddle and bid her ride as fast as she could and not Stop or Slack for me except I bad her and so I would run untill I was *much* out of breath; and then mount my horse again, and so I did several times to favour my horse; we improved every moment to get along as if we were fleeing for our lives; all the while fearing we would be too late to hear the Sermon, for we had twelve miles to ride double in little more than an hour and we went round by the upper housen parish.

> And when we came within about half a mile or a mile of the Road that comes down from Hartford weatherfield and Stepney to Middletown; on high land I saw before me a Cloud or fogg rising; I first thought it came from the great River, but as I came nearer the Road, I head a noise something like a low rumbling thunder and presently found it was the noise of Horses feet coming down the Road and this Cloud was a Cloud of dust made by the Horses feet; it arose some Rods onto the air over the tops of Hills and trees and when I came within about 20 rods of the Road, I could see men and horses Sliping along in the Cloud like shadows and as I drew nearer it seemed like a steady Stream of horses and their riders, scarcely a horse more than his length behind another, all of a Lather and Foam with sweat, their breath rolling out of their nostrils every Jump; every horse seemed to go with all his might to carry his rider to hear news from heaven for

the saving of Souls, it made me tremble to see the Sight, how the world was in a Struggle; I found a Vacence between two horses to Slip in mine and my Wife said law our Cloaths will be all spoiled see how they look, for they were so covered with dust, that they looked almost all of a Colour Coats, hats, Shirts, and Horses.

We went down in the Stream but heard no man speak a word all he way for 3 miles but every one pressing forward in great haste and when we got to Middletown old meeting house there was a great Multitude it was said to be 3 or 4000 of people Assembled together; we dismounted and shook off our Dust; and the ministers were then Coming to the meeting house; I turned and looked towards the Great River and saw the ferry boats Running swift backward and forward bringing over loads of people and the Oars Rowed nimble and quick; every thing men horses and boats seemed to be Struggling for life; the land and banks over the river looked black with people and horses all along the 12 miles I saw no man at work in his field, but all seemed to be gone.[1]

Whitefield's preaching was more powerful than even Cole had expected, touching off in him a spiritual crisis that nearly resulted in suicide. Even as worldly and skeptical a man as Benjamin Franklin was moved by Whitefield. When Franklin perceived that Whitefield intended to conclude his Philadelphia sermon with a collection, the old philosopher hardened himself against seduction: "I silently resolved he should get nothing from me." Franklin had in his pocket "a handful of copper money, three or four silver dollars, and five pistoles of gold."

As he proceeded I began to soften, and concluded to give the coppers. Another stroke of his oratory made me asham'd of that, and determin'd me to give the silver; and he finish'd so admirably, that I empty'd my pocket wholly into the collector's dish, gold and all.[2]

An anonymous contributor to the *New England Weekly* reported a similar experience in New York. Being possessed of "Scruples" and "Doubts" at the outset of Whitefield's sermon, he was nevertheless quickly impressed with what seemed to him a visible Presence of God within Mr. Whitefield. I came Home astonished. Every Scruple vanished. I never saw nor heard the like, and I said within myself, *Surely God is with this Man of Truth.*" Round the edges of this particular crowd groups of hecklers had gathered, "gigling, Scoffing, Talking and Laughing." But as Whitefield continued they fell silent: "a solemn Awe and Reverence appeared in the Faces of most, a mighty Energy attended the Word."[3]

Whitefield was the most prominent of the evangelists, but other ministers awakened the same sort of religious frenzy in their listeners. Jonathan Parsons, one of the leading revivalist preachers among the

Presbyterian clergy, awakened Presbyterians throughout the middle colonies. "I observed many of the Assembly in Tears," he wrote of one sermon, "and heard many crying out in a very great Bitterness of Soul. . . . " Some of his listeners fell into "Hysterick-Fits" during his preaching, while others

> had their Countenances changed; their thots' seemed to trouble them, so that the joynts of their Loyns were loosed, and their Knees smote one against another. Great Numbers cried out aloud in the Anguish of their Souls: several stout Men fell as tho' a Cannon had been discharged, and a Ball had made its' Way thro' their Hearts.[4]

Many slumbering Christians were rudely awakened by Whitefield and the other itinerate evangelists. But "awakening" was only the first step of a conversion scenario that included as many as ten steps.[5] Thus Nathan Cole, touched as deeply as he had been by Whitefield's preaching, required nearly two years of struggle, search and anguish before he experienced that infusion of grace that signified conversion and assurance. Itinerate evangelists may have sown the seeds of conversion, but the more lengthy and arduous task of harvesting fell upon the resident clergy. Thus Jonathan Parsons found that "a considerably Number" of people came to him after Whitefield's sermon "and confess'd that they saw themselves undone [and] earnestly enquired what they must do to be Saved, who dated their first Awakening from that Sermon." Parsons' regular communicants demanded more sermons, more evening lectures, more personal counseling, taxing the minister's physical endurance. At one point in 1744 Parsons reported that he was preaching nearly every day, that his assemblies were greater than ever before, and that many of those who attended his public preaching of the Word "were frequently in my Study for Advice."[6]

Samuel Blair, minister of the Church at New Londonderry in Pennsylvania, has left us a description of the intense interaction between minister and awakened that often followed upon the work of the itinerants. After a local evangelist preacher had "awakened" his congregation Blair discovered "an uncommon Teachableness" among them. He reported sobbing, fainting and "Strange unusual Bodily Motions" at public worship, but also a new attention to study of the Scriptures. "Excellent Books that had lain by much neglected, were then persu'd, and lent from one to another." Blair discovered that "the Subjects of Discourse almost always when any of them were together, were the Matters of Religion. . . . " He doubled his sermons through the summer of 1744, explaining "the awful Condition of such as were not in CHRIST, giving the Marks and Characters of such as were in that

Condition" and "laying open the Way of Recovery in the New Covenant." Blair "labour'd much" throughout the summer, encouraging some, admonishing others. Particularly difficult cases "obliged me to be at much Pains in my Enquiries before I cou'd get any just Ideas of their Case." Blair's customary procedure with such persons was to listen to their relations and then to conduct what he called "a thorough careful Examination" of their thoughts and feelings.

> I would ask them, what were the Thoughts, the Views, and Apprehensions of their Minds, and Exercise of their Affectations at such Times when they felt, perhaps, a quivering over come them, as they had been saying, or a Faintness, though they saw their Hearts full of some nautious Filthiness, or when they felt a heavy Weight and Load at their Hearts, or felt the Weight again taken off, and a pleasant Warmness rising from their Hearts, as they would probably express themselves, which might be the Occasions or Causes of these Things they spoke of? And then, when with some Difficulty I cou'd get them to understand me, some of them wou'd give a pretty rational Account of solemn Spiritual Exercises.[7]

Sensitive to the delicacy of this nurturing task, Blair was "all along very cautious" in his examinations: "Sometimes . . . I have thought it needful to use greater Freedom that Way than ordinary, but otherwise I judged that it could be of little Use, and might readily be hurtful." In such cases Blair devoted himself more to listening and encouraging than to examining.[8]

The thankfulness with which Blair greeted the Awakening, and the care and concern with which he nurtured the faithful in his own congregation, resulted not only in a "considerable Number" of lasting conversions, but as well in a sense of pleasure and delight that pervaded his church. "We enjoy in this Congregation," he reported, "the happiness of a great Degree of Harmony and Concord: Scarcely any have appear'd to open Opposition and Bitterness."[9]

II

Not all ministers were as receptive to the Awakening, or as anxious to cultivate and harvest its fruits. In the northern colonies an "Old Light Party" emerged which condemned the Awakening as "subversive of the Order of the Gospel and Peace of the Churches," and "tend[ing] to destroy the Interests of Christianity through Strifes and Divisions."[10] In Connecticut the Old Lights prevailed upon the legislature to pass a law in 1742 that prohibited itineracy, under punishment of fine and imprisonment. In Massachusetts the Old Lights assembled together in May of 1743 and condemned the Awakening as "most contrary to the Spirit and Precepts of the Gospel. . . . " Itineracy came in for special criticism as "an heinous Invasion of the ministerial Office, offensive to GOD, and destructive of these Churches. . . . "[11]   When Whitefield returned to the colonies in 1744 he found the pulpits of many churches shut tightly against him.

The leader of the Old Light Party in the northern colonies was Charles Chauncy, minister of Boston's First Church from 1727 to 1787. Chauncy was the first minister to publicly censure the Awakening, and throughout the 1740s he remained the Old Lights' most outspoken and prolific spokesman.   Yet his perceptions were thoroughly typical of the Old Lights. A close examination of the attitudes he displayed toward the Awakening will therefore serve to illustrate the temperament of the Old Lights generally and will also serve to distinguish it from the temperament of the Old Calvinists, whose perceptions of the Awakening will be discussed in the final section of this chapter.

In his character, Charles Chauncy combined enormous powers of self-application and a wonderful analytical ability with an almost total lack of intuitive imagination or sensibility.   "He had so little idea of poetry," a contemporary once remarked, "that he could never relish it, and wished some one would translate *Paradise Lost* into Prose, that he might understand it."[12] A recent biographer described him as "a man of the intellect, utterly distrusting the emotions as calculated to befog and pervert the mind. . . . "[13] The control under which he always kept himself can be glimpsed in this description of his daily regimen, offered by a friend shortly after Chauncy's death:

> The Doctor was remarkably temperate in his diet and exercise. At twelve o'clock he took one pinch of snuff, and only one in twenty-four hours. At one o'clock, he dined on one dish of plain, wholesome food, and after dinner took one glass of wine, and one pipe of tobacco, and only one in twenty-four hours. And he was equally methodical in his exercise, which consisted chiefly or wholly of walking.[14]

Restraint characterized his pulpit style too. By all available accounts he was a dull and tiring preacher. He regarded even the slightest rhetorical flourishes as compromises of intellectual integrity. One of his parishioners, upon learning that Chauncy had prayed that God would never make him an orator, dryly remarked that his prayer had been "unequivocally granted."[15]

By training too, Chauncy was a man of the intellect. His great-grandfather had served as the second president of Harvard College and Chauncy himself took both a BA and an MA from that institution. His teachers at Harvard had thought him "a Hopefull Young Scholar" and had encouraged him with scholarships and appointments. He served as

"Scholar of the House" at Harvard and, later, as a tutor there for six years. He sat on the Harvard Board of Overseers by virtue of his ministerial post and was a founding member of the American Academy of Arts and Sciences. By both nature and nurture, he was opposed to the evangelical impulse that underlay the Great Awakening.

Chauncy's theology was a natural extension of his character and training. In the 1730s he stood as one of the foremost proponents of proto-Arminian doctrines. He rejoiced in the softening of Calvinist dogma and in the increased latitude of thought and action this "decline" made possible. "Let us always plead for the *Use of Liberty* in the Affairs of our *Souls*, and *another World*," he once declared.[16] Believing that "we have no way of judging but by what is *outward* and *visible*," he abolished the practice of public testimony at the First Church and championed acceptance of the Half-Way Covenant. "It is worthy of our thankful Notice," he told his congregation in 1739, "that the principles of *Liberty* are every Day gaining Ground in our *Nation*," that the church "invades no Man's Right of Conscience, nor threatens him with Punishment for the greatest Difference of Judgment, in Matters of Religion." He thought it a matter of progress that " . . . even *Dissenters from Christianity itself*, have been suffered to enjoy and publish their Sentiments, without any other Opposition but that of Reason and argument."[17]

For Chauncy the essence of the evangelical challenge lay in the fact that it blurred together and collapsed the several phases of the conversion process into a single, dramatic and utterly subjective experience. This was not completely true, of course. Evangelical ministers insisted that "awakening" was not the same thing as conversion, that awareness of one's sinful and undone condition had to be followed by a regular attendance upon the Word, submission to the moral law, and doubt and despair before it could possibly issue in true sanctification and election. But it *is* true that they looked upon awareness of one's sinful condition and absolute dependence upon Christ as a subjective, extra-cognitive experience; that they placed primary importance upon this experience; that they developed sermon techniques which proved remarkably effective in generating such an experience; and that amongst their followers this initial, "awakening" phase seemed often to be immediately followed by the feelings of assurance and release that properly belonged to the final phases of sanctification. "Conviction of sin is a thing quite different from conversion," Chauncy reminded the evangelicals. "'Tis only the first step towards it, a *preparation of mind* making way for it:

Nor unless it end in this blessed change, will it signify anything, [even] if persons are under ever so deep distress"[18] (my emphasis).

Properly understood, man was preeminently a reasonable being, one whose religious growth came through study of the scriptures and a steady attendance upon the means ordained by God and instituted in the regularly established churches. The evangelical emphasis upon inward, subjective experience smacked to Chauncy of antinomianism and he criticized it as such. "Wherever he went," Chauncy said of Whitefield,

> he generally moved the *Passions* . . . *Mr. Whitefield's* Doctrine of *inward Feelings* began to discover itself in Multitudes, whose *sensible Perceptions* arose to such a Height, as that they *cried out, fell down, swooned away,* and, to all Appearances, were like Persons in Fits. . . . [19]

"The work of the SPIRIT," Chauncy countered, lies not in such inward experiences, but "in preparing men's *minds* for the grace of God. . . . It does not lie in giving men *private revelations,* but in opening their *minds* to understand the publick ones contained in the scripture."[20]

Chauncy did not mean to rule out all subjective experiences, but only to keep them properly subordinate to cognitive apprehension. "Human passions are capable of serving valuable purposes in religion," he acknowledged, "and may to good advantage be excited and warmed." But "always provided they are kept under the restraints of *reason*. . . . " The tragedy of the Great Awakening lay in its ignorance of proportion. "*Light* and *Heat* should always go together; and if there be not some good proportion of the former, it will turn to little account, if there be ever so much of the latter."[21]

Sometimes Chauncy took this line of thought even further, arguing that the sinfulness of which men must be made initially aware was the sin of subjective experience itself. "One of the most *essential* things necessary in the *new-forming* of men," he wrote in *Seasonable Thoughts,* "is the reduction of their *Passions* to a proper Regimen. . . ."[22] The revivalists "place their Religion so much in the *Heat* and *Fervour* of their *Passions,* that they too much neglect their *Reason* and *Judgement*."[23]

More objectionable to Chauncy than the revivalists' indulgence of subjectivity was their apparent manipulation of the sensibilities of their listeners. In order to generate the extra-cognitive experiences that were the acme of revivalism, the evangelical preachers had developed a sermon style that appealed directly to the fears and anxieties of their listeners. Jonathan Edwards went about this in a very self-conscious way, studying Locke's theory of the sensory apprehension of ideas and forming from it a sermon technique that, as Gilbert Tennent said in another context, "thrust the Nail of Terror into sleeping Souls."[24]

The result, from Chauncy's point of view, was an unleashing of primitive energies in the most violent way. In his *Letter from a Gentleman in Boston . . .* (1742) Chauncy offered a vivid description of this phenomenon.

> The Speaker delivers himself with the greatest Vehemence both of Voice and Gesture, and in the most frightful Language his Genius will allow of. If this has its intended Effect upon one or two weak Women, the Shrieks catch from one to another till a great Part of the Congregation is affected . . . some . . . cry out themselves, on purpose to move others and bring forward a general Scream. Visions now become Common, and Trances also, the Subjects of which were in their own Conceit transported from Earth to Heaven, where they saw and heard most glorious Things.[25]

What is most striking about this account is not the events themselves — we have seen similar events described by Parsons and Blair — but Chauncy's perception of manipulation as the determining element. He is describing, as he says, an "intended Effect." If you should once come under the influence of it," he warned, "none can tell whither it would carry you . . . your recovery to a right mind would be one of the most difficult things in nature."[26]

Just as the emphasis on subjective experience overwhelmed the rational faculties, so the manipulation of collective anxiety did violence to the uniqueness of each person's religious apprehension: ". . . the *passionate* part of this joy," Chauncy insisted, "is widely different in different persons." The danger with the revivals was that they tended to obscure these subtle differences, to bury them under the violence of public display. "*Force* is proper to the *Body*," Chauncy argued, "*Reason* to the *Mind.*"

> The *Use of Force*, in Matters of *Religion* . . . conveys no Light into the Mind; it brings no Conviction to the Judgement and Conscience, it effects no Alteration in Men's Thoughts and Sentiments . . . tis plainly inverting the Order of Nature, to make Use of that with Reference to the *Soul*, which is adapted, in its Use only to the Body . . . [27]

The importance that evangelical ministers attached to subjective experience not only undermined a proper understanding of religious experience but threatened social stability as well. In *Seasonable Thoughts,* Chauncy reminded his readers that the German peasants, persuaded by *"Visions, Raptures, and Revelations"* that "the Saints were now to reign on Earth," had actually taken up arms against the lawful authority. "Enthusiastic wildness has slain its thousands," he warned, and he feared its effects in New England. The revivals had made New

Englanders "*spiritually proud* and *conceited* beyond Measure, infinitely *censorious* and *uncharitable.*" "Things have been carried too far," he wrote in 1742. The Awakening "has promoted faction and contention; filled the church oftentimes with confusion, and the state sometimes with general disorder." Christians had begun "to bite and devour one another, injure and mal-treat each other." "Heats and Animosities" had arisen and issued, "in some places, to open divisions and separations." He even voiced a fear that attempts would be made "to destroy all property, to make all things common, *wives* as well as *goods.*" "Can you reflect upon this, and be easy in your mind?" he asked the revivalists. "Have you had no misgivings or fears? No inward relentings?"[28]

Chauncy had been the first of the New England ministers to speak out against the Awakening. For the rest of his life he regarded the passions released by the Awakening as the greatest threat facing civil society. Had he been a magistrate instead of a minister he would have used his authority to forcibly repress the revivals. In *Seasonable Thoughts,* he urged that the revivalists be treated as Winthrop had handled Anne Hutchinson and the antinomians a hundred years before.[29] In 1747 he warned Governor William Shirley and the assembled Council and House of Representatives of "dangerous enemies" in the community who sought, through "artful application," to arouse "the fears and jealousies of the people." In 1752 he proposed construction of a linen factory to employ the poor, whom he called "the main Source of that Variance and Strife which disturb the Peace of Society." As late as 1771, long after the animosities generated by the Awakening had subsided, he was railing against evangelical religion as "worse than paganism" and venting his fear that it would "undoe the Colony."[30]

III

In his book *Jonathan Edwards,* Perry Miller wrote that during the Great Awakening the New England clergy "divided itself in two, into 'New Light' and 'Old Light'. . . . " Similarly, in *The Great Awakening in New England,* Edwin Gaustad wrote that during the Awakening the clergy was "crystallized" into "parties," that "each minister found himself drawn away from a comfortable neutrality, to one of the opposing poles."[31]

In this interpretation, the Awakening is presented as a conflict over the past and future of New England church history. Both Old Lights and New Lights agreed that the established churches had largely abandoned the original and fundamental distinction between saints and sinners and had become very nearly parish churches. The New Lights rejected these compromises because they had brought the community to the communion table, transformed the Eucharist from a seal of election into a means of grace, and transmuted piety into moralism. They wanted to re-establish the spiritual communion of the saints, to recapture the Eucharist as an emblem rather than a means, and to revive the piety of the founders. This is the meaning that Jonathan Edwards and a few others saw in the Awakening. They tried to reverse the process of declension, to turn history back upon its own tracks, to recapture the past. From this perspective the key New Light document is not Edwards' *Original Sin*, but his *Humble Inquiry Into the Qualifications Requisite to . . . Full Communion* (1749), in which he explained his decision to limit communion to visible saints. The thrust of the Awakening, in any consistent sense, was to abolish the Half-Way Covenant. This is the meaning that Miller, Gaustad, Alan Heimert and others, following Edwards, have seen in the Great Awakening.

But most clergymen supported both the revivals and the standing order, aligning themselves with neither the New Lights nor with the Old Lights. It seems likely that their middle-of-the-road course through the Awakening was a course most New England clergymen followed, though this is difficult to verify. There is nothing unusual about this; in any age men find it convenient to ignore or gloss over the signs of irrevocable cleavage and change in their society. Most colonial ministers possessed neither the disposition nor the ability to see that the conflict between the Old Lights and the New Lights would ultimately break colonial religious culture in halves, that in the end there would be no middle ground.

Consider, for example, the middle-of-the-road course followed by Eliphat Adams, minister of the First Church of New London from 1709 until his death in 1753. Adams possessed all of the qualities that we usually associate with an Old Light: he was a well-read gentleman and he was pastor of a wealthy, liberal congregation; he preached a gentle, loving God and stressed the possibilities and rewards of virtue; he looked upon the common people as giddy and unreasonable, liable at any moment to be set in a flame; and against this fickle multitude he sought to extend and expand the prerogatives of the clergy. During the Great Awakening he was bitterly attacked by the New Lights; and he in turn had several of them arrested. At the same time, however, he sparked a revival in his own church and invited George Whitefield, Jonathan Parsons and other itinerants to help him bring in the spiritual harvest he had sown. In these ways his middle-of-the-road course through the revivals epitomizes the path followed by a large number of New England clergymen.[32]

By upbringing, demeanor and position, Adams was a gentleman. He was born into a prominent clerical family and raised in the highest circles in Massachusetts provincial life. He served as a trustee of Yale College; was appointed treasurer of the Connecticut missionary fund by the Governor and General Court; enjoyed the company of Governor Gordon Saltonstall, Timothey Cutler and other Connecticut worthies; and was regarded by them as "the standard-bearer of the conservative forces" in that province.[33]

Like most well-read provincial gentlemen, Adams inclined toward theological liberalism. He preached the necessity of good works and assured his parishioners that God would reward them in heaven according to the efforts they expended on earth.[34] In June of 1701 the Brattle Square Church in Boston, then the most liberal Congregational church in all of New England, gave Adams a unanimous call to settle as assistant to Benjamin Colman—a position he filled "to the great satisfaction of the congregation" for two-and-a-half years. The First Church of New London, where he finally settled, had operated under the Half-Way Covenant since 1671; Adams continued to expand both baptism and admission policies during his pastorate.[35]

Toward the people thus brought into his church, Adams displayed an ambivalence born of both compassion and wariness. On the one hand, he exhibited a sensitivity to their hardships not commonly heard from members of his class. In May of 1733, for example, he told the Governor and the General Court that the "times" had left the common people "not a little pinched with poverty." You must not wonder, he told them, "if their complaints reach unto your ears and you be burdened with their petitions." At the same time, perhaps because of this sensitivity, he constantly worried lest some demagogue should burst upon the scene and set this combustible material ablaze. In 1730 he expressed his fear that "cavillers and opposers" might impose themselves upon the "giddy and unstable people" and "raise a tumult." Four years later he reported that "an uneasie disposition hath been growing a long time" and said that he had been trying to figure out "which way this ferment in people's spirits will vent itself and what it will produce."[36]

The Great Awakening was first brought to New London by a series of itinerant New Lights early in 1741. Gilbert Tennent arrived on 30 March, preached three sermons that day, three the next, and then departed. James Davenport, the Southold itinerant gone berserk, appeared two months later, on 24 May, and touched off a week of riotous religious activity. On Friday 5 June Joshua Hempstead, a local Justice-of-the-Peace whose diary provides a full and revealing account of the Awakening in New London, recorded that the Davenport revivals had achieved "the greatest success imaginable and beyond what is rational to conceive of."[37]

Rather than try to quell this insurgent revivalism, as others of his standing and convictions were doing, Adams embraced it. He preached all day on Sunday 7 June and all day again the following Sabbath, bringing "about nine" adults into the church as full members. Two days later he introduced Joseph Parsons, the firebrand revivalist from Lyme, Connecticut, to preach from his pulpit.[38] On the Sunday following – 21 June – he again preached all day and brought "a great number above twenty" into full communion. Throughout the fall and into the winter Adams continued to preach, brought touring evangelists into his pulpit and gathered newly awakened persons into the church.   Always, Hampstead wrote in his diary, Adams' meeting house was packed, even when Davenport – as in the last two weeks in July – was screaming and yelling at the other end of town.[39]

At the same time, Adams was doing all he could to moderate and dampen the "excesses" that marred the revivals in New London. Some of Davenport's New London sermons were apparently hair-raising affairs, leaving "divers women . . . terified out exceedingly." After one particular sermon,

> Mr. Davenport dismist the congregation and some went into the broad allay which was much crowded and there he screamed out Come to Christ and Come away Come away . . . and there he held it Sometime singing and Sometime praying . . . and the women fainting . . . till 10 o'clock att night or thereabouts and then he went off singing.[40]

Early in July, Davenport set the people of New London "into a mighty ruffle and disturbance" when he publically attacked Adams, called him unregenerate, and offered up prayers for his mother, who had by then been sixty years in her grave.[41]

Five months after this incident, in November 1741, Adams attended a meeting of local clergymen called to deal with the rash of separations that had occurred in the New London area, and also with the "traveling ministers" who promoted them. By mid-1742 exhorters operating in New London were being systematically arrested and imprisoned, and in July the ministers and magistrates of that city met to deal with itinerants. By attending and supporting these meetings – he hosted one of them – Adams indicated that his support for the revivals was qualified, that he would join in repressing those enthusiasts who threatened to disrupt existing institutions.[42]

We can glimpse Adams' "middle way" one final time, in the summer of 1745. On 16 June of that year a group of New Light exhorters "came to ye meetinghouse and began to preach"; Adams responded by having them immediately arrested and imprisoned. Then, less than two months later, Whitefield, the Grand Itinerant himself, passed through New London on his way to Georgia. Adams invited him to the First Church and beamed while Whitefield addressed "a grate assembly" from Adams' own pulpit.[43]

Adams' middle-of-the-road course through the Awakening epitomized the experience of many New England divines who aligned themselves neither with the Old Lights nor with the New Lights. Moreover, his motivations—or what we can see of something so murky and elusive—were also, in all probability, typical. I think that he was attracted to the middle path he followed for two reasons, one rather practical, the other having to do with ideals. Consider the practical problem first, the problem of declining church attendance. During the 1730s, as we saw in the preceding chapter, Adams complained that his people were not coming to church, that he had to "go after them into the mountains and thickets." If the revivals did nothing else, they boosted sagging church attendance for those ministers willing to participate. Hempstead testified that during the 1740s Adams preached to a meetinghouse that was continually full. A middle path like the one Adams followed must have seemed the only path open to men who were wary of popular sentiment but worried by declining church attendance.

Second, consider the role of balance as an ideal in colonial New England thought. It had been the lodestone of seventeenth century Calvinism and in the eighteenth century it became in different form the watchword of what Henry May has called "the Moderate Enlightenment." Men argued about exactly where that balance lay, of course; but for all, the ideal of balance whether expressed in philosophical, religious or political terms, remained paramount. And along with most eighteenth century divines, Adams repeated over and again, like a litany, his commitment to balance. "We must carefully avoid both the extreams," he warned in 1730. "We must not run into enthusiasm and impute every whim and notion and odd impression to the Spirit of God . . . Nor yet on the other hand must we deny to acknowledge its actual occurence. . . . " The ideal of balance must have inhibited men from taking up either outright advocacy of, or opposition to, the revivals.

The vast majority of New England ministers passed over the Awakening without any printed comment at all. When they did comment they usually expressed mixed reactions. The Reverend Nathaniel Appleton's response was typical of the way many New England clergymen approached the Awakening. Appleton was educated at Harvard and was minister of the Congregational Church in Cambridge from 1717 until his death in 1784. Unlike Chauncy, he did not believe that Christians were only to be addressed through their reason. "If the Preacher be wise so as to win Souls," he would seek not only to instruct the rational mind but to "move the Passions" of his listeners and cause them "to water the Word with their own Tears." He thus looked with favor on George Whitefield's preaching when Whitefield toured the colonies in 1740.[44]

Piety had suffered a decline at Appleton's church before Whitefield's arrival in 1740. The previous two years especially had been "but a dead and dull Time with us . . . "

> But blessed be God, there seems now some Revival among us; there are more affected, awakened, and convinced, and put upon their Duty, than is common among us. The Word preached seems to have come with greater Power upon the Souls of People, especially to the younger Sort.

Appleton also testified that most of those newly awakened "have declared to me, what powerful Influence his fervent Preaching had upon them."[45]

But Appleton's praise was restrained and cautious: there only *seems* to be an awakening; Whitefield's preaching only *seems* to have come with greater power. "Let us all be concerned," he urged his congregation, "that . . . there may be not only the Appearance, but a real Increase."

> We had need therefore take great Care in this Matter, because this is a case wherein we are apt to be deceived . . . there is often times that which looks like increase, and that promises fair for a glorious Harvest, but alas! it sinks away and comes to nothing . . . The Tears quickly dry-up, the warm affections presently cool, the Convictions suddenly go off, and the good Purposes don't last long enough for an Opportunity to put them into Practice.[46]

This concern was very different from the condemnation offered by Chauncy. Appleton was not critical of the Awakening, nor did he doubt that it was a work of God. In the same book from which the remark above was taken, Appleton wrote, "Mr. WHITEFIELD has watered, and GOD has given some Increase." And he offered his own "fervent Prayers for further Increase." His chief concern was that the revival of spirituality actually produce lasting conversions among his people. His attitude was one of caution rather than reaction, as can be seen in the following remark:

> We may and ought to rejoice and be thankful whenever we perceive the Word to take any Effect, and see by the powerful preaching of it, Convictions stirred up, and People concerned about their spiritual State . . . yet we may by no Means pronounce certainly concerning them at present . . . but must wait to see what Fruit they bring forth . . . instead of being too positive, or too confident of your

safe Estate by Reason of some convictions . . . I would advise you to a surer sign, and what may be more safely depended on, and that is your bringing forth Fruit with Patience.[47]

Andrew Eliot, minister of Boston's New North Church from 1742 until 1778, displayed the same cautious attitude toward the Awakening. Like Appleton he is usually regarded as an Arminian by historians. But like Appleton he understood the need "to preach with warmth and Earnestness. . . . " He called the doctrines of Calvinism "the very Life and Soul of Religion" and urged his fellow ministers to "dwell much upon them," even though they "may disgust the carnal Part of [the] Audience, and the polite Taste of the Age." And also like Appleton, Eliot welcomed Whitefield and the Awakening in 1740. To see "such Numbers. . . flying to JESUS as on a Cloud, and as Doves to their Windows . . . must make a faithful Minister go about his work with double Pleasure." Eliot offered his thanks "for the wonders [God] has of late wrought among us," urged "those who are under Awakenings" to seek him out for counsel, and assured them that "I shall rejoice in giving you all the advice and Assistance I am able."[48]

But like Appleton, Eliot was cautious in his approach to the Awakening and reticent to give it his unqualified endorsement. He criticized the censorious attitude that many of the newly awakened directed toward the standing clergy and he warned them against "the prejudice we are under, with respect to doctrines which we think true," especially those "which had been deeply impressed on our minds when first we entered on the Christian life."

> We are ready to think all religion consists in these, and that he is a stranger to vital Christianity who doth not embrace them, or fall in with our explication of them. Whereas, it is possible we may be mistaken, things may appear very differently to others as upright as ourselves, and the same desireable effect may be produced by sentiments not, in every respect, consonant to ours.[49]

Eliot's attitude toward the Awakening was best revealed in his counseling of newly awakened persons. On the one hand he was pleased to see so many members of his congregation awakened by Whitefield's preaching, so many "in a fair Way of escaping eternal Misery." He was acutely aware of what he called "the Need of much Skill and Wisdom" in counseling "poor awakend Soules," and sought to avoid "any thing which should any way obstruct their eternal Happiness." On the other hand he thought that most ministers were "too apt to have [their] tender Passions raised" by seeing their communicants withering in spiritual agony, "and so . . . alleviate their Sorrow by affording them too much

Encouragement." His solution was "not [to] immediately apply Comfort" until he could "search the Wound to the Bottom" for evidence of a lasting conversion.[50]

Eliot's refusal to align himself with either of the Awakening's contending factions occasionally roused the ire of both New Lights and Old Lights. He was roundly and publicly attacked by the Old Lights for allowing George Whitefield to preach a series of lectures in the New North Church in 1770, and criticized by the New Lights when he invited the Liberal William Emerson into his pulpit the following spring.[51]

Other moderates displayed the same independence of mind. Consider the case of Solomon Williams, minister of the church at Lebanon, Connecticut from 1721 to 1776. Williams is usually regarded as an Arminian. He followed an extremely liberal policy on admission to communion and baptism, preached a loving and gentle God, and maintained personal friendships with many of the leading Arminians, including Chauncy. Nevertheless, he welcomed the Awakening as a revival of traditional piety, opened his church to Whitefield when he toured the colonies in 1744, and more often than not voted with the New Lights in his capacity as a trustee of Yale College. In 1742 he simultaneously criticized both the Connecticut legislature's anti-itineracy legislation and what he regarded as the excesses of the New Lights. Because of his refusal to side with either of the contending religious factions he was often called upon to mediate conflicts between them. In this role his evenhanded temperment and his disposition to compromise stood him in good stead. A contemporary testified that Williams was "an Instrument of healing as many Breaches, and reconciling as many Differences as perhaps any man in his day," and called him "a Peace-maker in the true Gospel Sense."[52]

Like Eliot, Williams occasionally was attacked by both sides. The New Lights censured him for his perception of God as a loving and forgiving figure and for his practice of admitting persons to communion and baptism without a relation of conversion. The Old Lights criticized him for allowing Whitefield to preach in the Lebanon church and later vetoed Williams' appointment as a professor of Divinity at Yale College.[53]

Like Appleton, Eliot and Williams, the Reverend Ezra Stiles has often been called an Arminian; Edmund Morgan thought him "something more, a child of the Enlightenment," and has tentatively suggested that he "would appear to have been a deistic Christian."[54] Suffice it to say that he was closer to the Arminians than he was to the evangelicals. He championed acceptance of the Half-Way Covenant and he dispensed with public testimony as a requirement for admission to his

Newport church, admitting into communion all who professed a belief in Christian principles and seemed free of extraordinary sin. "It is really impossible for us to judge of the Heart," he wrote. "The blameless and sober Life, is all we can judge of." Indeed, Stiles' religion hardly seems to have been an affair of the heart at all: "I became a Christian rather as a Believer in a well imagined and most beautiful moral System," he admitted, "than as feeling the Evidence of a certain real derivation from God." He once told his friend Jared Ingersoll that, "I intend, when I have got a little more *moral cash*, to travel largely in the Almighty's Dominions." "I shall never be a New Light," he admitted in 1761.[55]

And like others of his temperament he criticized the antics of the more fervent New Lights. Speaking to a convention of clergymen in 1760, he condemned "the unhappy excesses . . . the mistaken public zeal . . . [the] extravagancies and indecencies . . . into which our churches have been transported. . . ."

> Multitudes were seriously, soberly and solemnly out of their wits. The scriptures were in danger of being neglected for the indistinguishable impulses of the spirit of God; sober reason gave way to enthusiasm; the terrors of eternal damnation, instead of subserving rational and sober convictions, were improved to throw people into that confusion, frenzy and distraction, which unfitted them for the genial illuminations of the holy spirit.[56]

Though he criticized such excesses, he maintained a tolerant, even interested attitude toward the Awakening as a whole. When Whitefield returned for his third visit to America in 1770, Stiles invited him to preach from his pulpit and entertained him at his home. Even more revealing was his encounter with the Separatist Joseph Snow the following summer. Joseph Snow was a house carpenter who had been awakened during Whitefield's 1744 itinerary. Two years later Snow led a large separation from his Providence, Rhode Island, Congregational church—a separation so large that it nearly destroyed the church. Snow and his followers then joined a group of local Baptists and, as Stiles told it, "formed themselves into a mixt and distinct Chh, and Elected Mr. Snow Pastor." Stiles found a great deal to criticize in this episode: the separation itself, the lay-ordination of Snow, adult baptisms, lay-exhorting, and most distressing of all, an "inveterate Displeasure against the old Congregational Chhs and Pastors." Snow himself seemed "loud and boisterous," taken to "running about into Congregational parishes in opposition to the Pastors, and holding separate meetings and promoting a spirit of Disaffection to a learned Ministry." Distasteful as these things were, Stiles also found a great deal to appreciate in this minister and his church. He took the trouble to visit and talk with Snow and found him, for all his illiteracy and "peculiarities," to be a "sober, serious, exemplary" man possessed of "many sound Truths." Stiles thought the church covenant that bound together Snow's congregation a good one and took the time to write out a complete copy for his own use. Stiles concluded his account of this episode with the remark that "I hope he does good."[57]

Still another episode, occurring about the same time, involved both Stiles and Chauncy and therefore serves to illustrate their contrasting attitudes toward the New Lights. In the winter of 1770 Samuel Hopkins accepted a call from the First Congregational Church at Newport. Stiles had then been settled at the Second Church for fifteen years. Hopkins had studied under Jonathan Edwards and had achieved a certain notoriety by preaching a pre-destinarian Calvinism even harsher than his mentor's.[58] When Chauncy heard of Hopkins' pending settlement he sent his friend Stiles a letter. "I'm sorry, with my whole soul that Mr. Hopkins is like to settle at Newport," he wrote. "I have a much worse opinion of his principles than of Sandeman's." A month later he wrote Stiles another letter, again expressing sympathy with the distress he imagined Stiles must have felt having a man of such seemingly backward principles preaching so near by. This time he was emphatic: he called Hopkins "a troublesome, conceited, obstinate man" who was "disposed inflexibly to destroy true religion," and told Stiles that he knew "of no worse system of thot in any pagan nation, in any age, than is publickly professed by [him]."[59]

Stiles did not share Chauncy's alarm. "I have a mind," Stiles wrote his father-in-law, "that there should be one Instance on the Continent, where two Churches in the same place and of the same Denominations would live in harmony. In most Instances they hate one another most heartily." And he was as good as his word. He preached the sermon at Hopkins' installation service, regularly attended his evening lectures, and in 1771 embarked with him upon a scheme to train local black people for missionary work in Africa. Though Hopkins was, in Edmund Morgan's estimation, "as opinionated as a man can be," Stiles and Hopkins became close and warm friends.[60]

The key to understanding Stiles' attitude toward the New Lights, and toward the Awakening in general, lies in his truly remarkable and unbounded curiosity. In a thoroughly typical week in March, 1773, for example, he recorded in his Diary his thoughts and observations upon the following:

  – "the number of Souls in Newfoundland"
  – the transits of Venus and Mercury
  – "Congregational Accounts from the Moravian Missionaries in Egypt."

- the "first volume of the Turkish Spy"
- the pronunciation of various sounds in the Arabic language (he eventually acquired a reading and speaking ability in Arabic)
- the growth of the Church of England in the Southern colonies
- the number of Indians in North America ("that is, from the Mississippi to the Atlantic Ocean, and from Florida to the Pole.")

Demography particularly interested him. "I intend," he wrote in the middle of that week, "to investigate the population of the *Mongul, Calmuk, &c. Tartars*: so as to form a more just Estimate of all the Inhabitants upon the Earth." He ended the week with a visit from "the Rabbi," whom he failed to name but described as "a large man, neat and well dressed in the Turkish Habit." They discussed, according to Stiles' Diary " . . . the Gemara, the 2 Talmuds [Stiles preferred the Babylonish], the Changes of the Hebrew Language in different Ages, &c. &c."[61]

This inveterate curiosity was important because it gave Stiles a deep appreciation of cultural and religious diversity, a quality utterly missing from Chauncy's character. In his mid-twenties Stiles began visiting the services of various denominations and sects in the northern and middle colonies (including those of the Roman Catholics and Jews) and continued this practice throughout his life. After visiting a Baptist meeting or a Jewish service—he thought Newport fortunate to have one of the country's few Jewish communities—Stiles would hurry home and record everything he could remember of the experience, including the meaning and significance of particularly interesting episodes. He also kept an account of the different nationalities that entered the northern- and middle-colony ports, writing down national characteristics that seemed to him especially remarkable.[62]

It was out of his curiosity, his intense fascination with the diversity of life, that his attitude toward the Awakening sprang. "Men build their houses differently," he once wrote,

> cultivate their lands differently, pursue the same employments in different methods, and in different methods study the sciences . . . [thus an] empire consists of a multitude of cities, burroughs, town and provinces, differently constituted by accident, according to the different geniuses of the people consociated.[63]

Similarly in religious affairs: "If different usages and customs in ecclesiastical polity are finally settled in different churches, this need not disturb the general harmony. . . [for] coercive uniformity is neither necessary in politics nor religion."[64]

There was a particular temperament or character made especially obvious against the backdrop of the Great Awakening that clearly distinguished what were to become the Old Calvinists from the evangelical Calvinists on their left and the Arminian Calvinists on their right. During the late 1750s and early 1760s that temperament was to find systematic expression in a body of theological ideas that is the concern of the next chapter.

The Theology of Old Calvinism

By 1750 the turmoil and contentions of the Great Awakening had largely subsided. Yet the decade that followed was regarded by many of the New England ministers as even more threatening than the previous one. From his post at Yale College, President Clap warned in 1755 that New England was threatened with nothing less than "the total Subversion of Christianity. . . . Since the Reformation the Gospel never met with more violent Opposition than at this time." At Newport, Rhode Island, Ezra Stiles voiced his alarm at "the minute philosophers initiated in the polite Mysteries and vitiated morals of Deism" that seemed to be springing up everywhere. "Make no doubt," he warned, "instead of the Controversies of Orthodoxy and Heresy, we shall soon be called to the defense of the Gospel itself." At Saybrook, William Hart warned his congregation to "guard ourselves against . . . the Deists of the present day," who, he said, "judge the Scriptures a cunningly devised Fable."[1]

Moderate-minded Calvinists took the lead in organizing New England Calvinism against this threat from Deism and Natural Religion. The fact that they had aligned themselves with neither the New Lights nor the Old Lights in the controversies of the 1740's, and the fact that they frequently mediated the conflicts between them, gave these men an excellent opportunity to reunite New England Calvinism in the troubled 1750s and 1760s. The task confronting them was a difficult one: to reformulate the principles of New England Calvinism in such a way as to exclude spiritism without cutting off evangelical Calvinism; and to exclude Deism and Natural Religion while incorporating New England's proto-Arminianism.

Ultimately they were unsuccessful. Old Calvinism survived into the nineteenth century only in the isolated writings of a small group of theologians clustered around the Princeton Divinity School. Nineteenth-century Protestantism was more significantly shaped by the divergence of precisely those forces Old Calvinism had tried to hold in balance — evangelicalism and rationalism.

But from the perspective of the third quarter of the eighteenth century they were successful. It was largely on the basis of theological and ecclesiastical principles articulated by the Old Calvinists that New England Calvinists united to oppose first the expansion of Anglican authority in the 1760s and then British administrative authority in the 1770s. Stiles' *Discourse on the Christian Union*, first published in 1761, went through several printings and two different editions, earning more money than any sermon in New England's history. Even Charles Chauncy thought it "so well adapted" that he offered to help Stiles distribute the pamphlet.[2]

Even more important were the emotional energies unleashed by this drive to renew the principles of New England Calvinism. The sense of redemption that underlay the revolutionary movement sprang largely from the Old Calvinists' effort to return to the first principles of New England Calvinism, to recapture and renew the legacy of the founding generation. Stiles' *Discourse on the Christian Union* conveys a vivid sense of the momentum and expectancy that this movement of renewal had generated by 1760. "We are nearly recovered to the purity of the primitive apostolic churches," Stiles exclaimed. "The next capital change will be to a still greater purity both in doctrine and worship." When the church had been prostituted by papal corruption God had "raised up and spirited the Reformation. . . ." "But to me," Stiles declared, "it appears He has reserved the honor of a most purified reformation for our churches in New-England."[3]

I

The essence of Calvinism had always been in its particular perception of the human condition. This was as true in New England as in Europe, and it was this perception that underlay and informed the theology of Old Calvinism and that most clearly and radically distinguished it from Natural Religion and Deism.

For those attracted to Natural Religion, man seemed not depraved but a manifestation of divine excellence. "To say that [God] gives mortal beings as we are a nature which . . . is odius to Him," Samuel Webster wrote in 1757, "is contrary to all His perfections." Rather it seemed, as William Smith explained in 1755, "that God made us for Happiness." Not that God *saved* us *to* happiness, but that He *made* us *for* happiness, that "we were *designed* for social life," that the "inward Furniture of our Nature" inclines us to happiness, both our own and that of others. Men are "by Nature both fitted and disposed to encrease each other's Happiness." And natural man possessed not only an inclination to happiness and social intercourse, but as well a mind capable of piercing the deepest secrets of life, of "follow[ing] truth in all her labyrinths . . . and thus lay[ing] the foundation of an eternal improvement in knowledge and happiness."[4]

Not many clergymen went this far. Most of those who were dissatisfied with the Calvinist image of human nature merely denied the idea of innate depravity, substituting in its place a Lockean image of mental emptiness as the "natural" condition of pre-social man. In 1759 Ebenezer Gay testified to the immense popularity of Lockean psychology among the colonial literati:

> The opinion of innate ideas and principles, which prevailed for so long a time, is now almost universally given-up; and that of the human mind receiving them afterwards distinct and simple; comparing, compounding and disposing of them, together with the perception of those operations, is adopted in its room, as the original of knowledge.[5]

The Old Calvinists rejected this easy view of man's estate. What they posited instead was the belief, in Stiles' words, that "we are now in a fallen and universally depraved state." This was a careful formulation that appealed to both evangelicals and Arminians because it left the *cause* of man's depravity unspecified. Evangelical Calvinists were free to find the cause in original sin, while the Arminians could simply take the formulation as a statement of fact. For although the Arminians had abandoned the doctrine of original sin, they had not adopted the optimistic view of man advocated by the Deists. The Old Calvinists' formulation appealed to the Arminians because it expressed their perception of man as a passionate being whose reasoning powers were too apt to be overwhelmed, in the Reverend Andrew Eliot's words, by "the enticements and temptations of an evil world." Eliot believed man to be "an intelligent creature . . . He is capable of thinking and reflecting, of judging of truth and falsehood, of distinguishing between right and wrong." But, he continued, "reason is blinded by a thousand passions, and we often act in direct contradiction to it." This perception was central to the Arminian persuasion. It determined their response to the upheavals of the Great Awakening and it continued in the 1750s and 1760s to shape their estimation of man's possibilities.[6]

Moreover, to the Arminians, knowledge was not something one acquired as a natural complement, like toes or fingers. Knowledge was something that one acquired only slowly, through discipline and self-application. True wisdom, one Arminian wrote,

> is not ordinarily to be acquired without hard Labour, and much Study, which exhausts the Spirits; and as Solomon tells us, is a weariness to the flesh.[7]

Whatever the source and nature of wisdom, evangelical and Arminian could agree that man's nature made its acquisition a struggle.

> Those men, who talk in such high strains of the light of nature, and who affirm with so much confidence that all "even the most ignorant and illiterate of the human race, have naturally and necessarily a clear and intimate perception of the whole of religion and their duty," forget that they were once children, and by what gradual steps they arrived to the degree of knowledge, to which they have attained, and of which they are so ready to boast.[8]

The Old Calvinist statement of human depravity was therefore a politic one, designed to win support from both evangelicals and Arminians while isolating Deism and Natural Religion. Stiles summarized the issue succinctly:

> Some may attribute it to vicious example, some to the disorder of our external state, or the animal part of man, some to a principle of pollution born in us, and derived from Adam. But however we may vary in our opinions as to the *cause* of the present reigning universal depravity, yet . . . I suppose we agree . . . that it is a fact . . . the universality of the effect shows a tendency and proclivity in our nature at present, however derived there.[9] (My emphasis)

II

The idea that Arminians asserted the efficacy of good works in the drama of man's salvation while evangelicals insisted that man is saved by faith alone has become commonplace among historians of eighteenth-century American thought. But this distinction is overdrawn; the difference between them was one of degree and emphasis. This was especially true after the initial enthusiasm of the Awakening had passed. On the one hand the evangelicals, frightened by "the unexpected and twisted channels of Antinomianism and Separatism" which the Awakening had opened up, attempted to shift the revivals' emphasis from immediate experience to the "fruits" of experience. On the other hand, the Arminians, similarly frightened by the appearance of Deism and Natural Religion in their midst, reaffirmed the necessity of divine grace in the act of salvation. The result was a closing of ranks around the orthodox belief that man is saved not *by* good works but *to* good works, that good works were not the cause of election but its fruits, although the doctrine underwent certain modifications, as we shall see.

In a remarkable essay that appeared in Boston in 1744, Experience Mayhew, father of the famous Jonathan Mayhew, described the position occupied by the most extreme of the evangelical Calvinists on the question of regeneration. The evangelicals, according to Mayhew,

> hold that true saving Conversion, which they also call Regeneration, is a great
> Change wrought in the Soul of a Sinner by the Spirit of God, whereby he has a
> new Biass or Disposition given him . . . And this they think is an *Instantaneous
> Change*; and that the Soul is passive in it . . . that it is wholly a Work of God
> by his Holy Spirit . . . Add hereunto, that, according to [evangelical] Calvinists,
> Sinners can do no Actions that are spiritually good, or truly holy, 'till this Change
> be first wrought in them; and consequently, it is impossible . . . that any Sinner
> should perform the Condition on which Salvation is offered to him, 'till he is first
> *converted and born of the Spirit*, as is above expressed.[10]

Arminians, in Mayhew's words, "think this Doctrine is so harsh they cannot endure it." What they found most objectionable in the formulation was the assertion 1) that regeneration was "an Instantaneous Change"; and 2) that "the soul is passive in it." Yet these were exactly the points which the evangelicals themselves moved most quickly to modify and moderate.[11]

Two years after Mayhew had published *Grace Defended*, Jonathan Edwards brought out his *Treatise Concerning Religious Affections . . .* (Boston, 1746). In this book Edwards sought to restrain the spiritism that had been unloosed by the Awakening. He acknowledged that "in the late extraordinary season" a great many apparent conversions had "come to nothing," that "some who seemed to be mightily raised and swallowed up with joy and zeal, for a while, seem to have returned like the dog to his vomit." The problem, Edwards contended, was not to condemn every form of affection in religious exercises but "to distinguish between affections, approving some, and rejecting others; separating between the wheat and the chaff, the gold and the dross, the precious and the vile."[12]

The distinguishing mark of a truly holy regeneration, Edwards contended, was not in the nature or intensity of the conversion event itself, for this may be merely "some extrordinary powerful influence of Satan . . . ," but rather in the way such an experience affected one's behavior.

> Indeed the power of godliness is exerted in the first place within the soul, in the
> sensible, lively exercise of gracious affections there. Yet the principle evidence of
> this power of godliness, is in those exercises of holy affections that are practical,
> and in their being practical; in conquering the will, and conquering the lusts and
> corruptions of men, and carrying men on in the way of holiness, through all
> temptations, difficulty, and opposition.[13]

Edwards was insisting that conviction of one's sinful and dependent state (the conversion event) did not immediately and necessarily result in true regeneration. At best it merely gave men and women the "Grace to endeavour to obey God's commandments." That this was a process of gradual growth can be perceived in the metaphor Edwards used:

> False discoveries and affections do not go deep enough to reach and govern the spring of men's actions and practice. The seed in stony ground had not deepness of earth, and the root did not go deep enough to bring forth fruit. But gracious affections go the very bottom of the heart, and take hold of the very inmost spring of life and activity.[14]

This position was similar to the position that the Old Calvinists and many of the Arminians had come to during the Awakening. "By their Fruits we shall know the Spirits which influence our Minds," William Hart had written in 1743.

> True Conversion supposes, that in Consequence of this Renovation of the Tempers of our Minds, there does follow, a thorou' Reformation of our Lives, and a regular habitual Practice of *all* the virtues of the Christian Life, . . . when this is wanting, there is Certainly, no true Conversion; whatever secret and high Experiences and Testimonies of the Spirit, . . . such persons may attend to. . . . [15]

Similarly, as early as 1741 Nathaniel Appleton had warned his congregation against "being too positive, or too confident" in the holiness of their conversion, but rather to insist upon what he called "a surer sign. . . . and that is your bringing forth Fruit with Patience, or Perseverence."[16] As on the question of original sin, Stiles summed up the "middle way," the political resolution to this part of the problem of regeneration, in his *Discourse on the Christian Union.* Speaking to evangelical Calvinists and Arminians, Stiles argued: " . . . it is only such a living faith as influences virtue, which is justifying."[17]

The second part of the problem of regeneration concerned the supposed passivity of the soul. By 1750 even the most fervent of the New Lights had abandoned this position. Joseph Bellamy was a student of Edwards' and one of the leaders of the New Light party in Connecticut. His *True Religion Delineated . . .* appeared in Boston in 1750 and was recognized as one of the major New Light statements of the post-Awakening period. In this work Bellamy was mainly concerned to deny the efficacy of good works in effecting regeneration—"to prevent the self from raising itself up as a rival to God." The heart of the book was Bellamy's strident insistence that even fulfillment of the covenant commandment—to love God with all thy heart and with all thy soul—was meaningless if it flowed from a self-conscious fear of damnation. "That seeming love," Bellamy wrote,

> which arises merely from selfish considerations, from the fear of punishment or hope of reward, or because the law requires it, and so it is a duty and must be

done, is not genuine, but is a selfish, a mercenary, and a forced thing . . . Such know not God.[18]

Regeneration comes neither from the conscientiousness of the formalist, nor from the joy, zeal and devotion of the "proud enthusiast," but only from what Bellamy called "Evangelical Humiliation," by which he meant "a sense of our own sinfulness, vileness, odiousness, and ill desert, and [from] a disposition thence resulting to lie down in the dust full of self-loathing and self-abhorrence, abased before the Lord." Though one could not expect to be saved by good works, one *could* be saved through Evangelical Humiliation:

> . . . through Christ, God, the supreme Gouvernor of the world, is actually ready to be reconciled, and invites all, the vilest not excepted, to return to him in this way.[19]

It is important to see that this represented not only a departure from formalism, but from enthusiasm as well. Indeed, Bellamy seems at times to regard the latter as a greater danger than the former. "Of all men in the world," Bellamy wrote, "I am ready to think that God looks upon these worst, and hates them the most." The notion of Evangelical Humiliation condemns

> . . . the faith of the proud enthusiast, who appears so good in his own eyes; so far from a legal spirit; so purely evangelical; so full of light and knowledge, humility and love, zeal and devotion . . . as that they rather feel more fit to be mediators and intercessors in behalf of others, than to want one for themselves . . . But there is nothing of the nature of true holiness in [them], for it is self, and nothing but self, that is the principal centre, and end of all their religion.[20]

Bellamy may have been more rigid than most of his New Light colleagues, but his notion of "Evangelical Humiliation," and his insistence that God stood ready to receive those who came to him in true humility, exerted a powerful influence in the post-Awakening period.

Old Calvinists and Arminians did not emphasize the need for humiliation of the kind Bellamy urged upon his listeners. But like him, they articulated a theory of regeneration that focused upon the necessity of sinners *coming* to Christ, actively searching Him out, without infringing upon God's sovereignty in deciding who would be saved and who would not. Where Bellamy urged "Evangelical Humiliation," the Old Calvinists and Arminians urged a constant and steady attendance upon the "means" to salvation offered in New England's established churches. "Although God can work above [the] Means, and without [the] Means," Nathanial Appleton explained, "yet it is not his ordinary Way:

He has appointed the Means, and he expects to be waited upon in the Way of those Means."

> We all know the Heat of the Sun gives Life and Power to the Seed to Grow: But does any Man expect to see his Field flourish with standing Corn, unless it be sown or planted? Nor more can you expect to see a divine Life begotten in your Souls, unless you diligently attend on the Word and Ordances.[21]

Not that such attendance alone would assure one's salvation. "Many people are apt to deceive themselves," Appleton warned, "and think they are near the kingdom of Heaven: yea, that they are actually in the kingdom of grace, because they are constant in attending religious worship . . . " Actual regeneration required, "first of all, a very deep sense of our lost and wretched state by reason of sin; and of our own utter inability to help or save ourselves . . . " But, Appleton continued,

> We are not to make the distinction so wide between the instituted means of grace, and the grace itself, as to neglect the means, under a pretence that we are looking after the end, the substantial parts of religion . . . although these duties may not be rested in, yet they must be observed by us.[22]

Many Old Calvinists and Arminians believed that preparation for regeneration was an essentially intellectual task, an attempt by the sinner to gain a rational, cognitive understanding of the truths contained in scripture. "Except we do truly understand and firmly believe the great Doctrines of the Gospel," William Hart warned,

> they can have no renewing, quickening and purifying influence upon our Hearts . . . The truth must first shine into the Understanding, must first be understood, believed and approved . . . before the Heart can be renewed . . . That religion cannot possibly be True, which is seated only in the Imagination and Passions, and not founded in an effectual Knowledge of the important Truths of the Gospel, and directed and influenced by a just Understanding and Belief of them . . . [23]

Hart called it "a high and foolish Presumption" to expect regeneration "while we neglect the Study of the written Word."

But neither did Hart believe that cognitive knowledge alone could justify sinners in the sight of God. We "can expect Pardon and Regeneration," Hart told his congregation,

> only from the free and Sovereign Grace of God, through the Atonement and Mediation of Jesus Christ . . . that we thus pray to God to regenerate us by his Spirit and Truth, is very necessary. For except God teach us by his Spirit, we shall never be able, by the mere exercise of our natural Powers, and use of the

standing Revelation of the Bible, to gain a renewing and saving Knowledge of God and Jesus Christ . . . [24]

Knowledge of the scriptures was thus a form of preparation, just as was Bellamy's "Evangelical Humiliation" and Appleton's attendance upon the "means":

> though our natural Reason alone is not sufficient for this purpose. [Hart wrote in 1742] Yet He does not teach us in such a Manner as to render the exercise of our own Reason Useless in our discovering the truth as it is in Jesus . . . The exercise of our natural reason is not therefore at all the less necessary to our coming to the saving knowledge of the Truth, because it is by the Spirit's teaching that we do learn it. [25]

By 1760, then, evangelicals and Arminians had come to a roughly similar understanding of man's role in the regeneration process. Both groups agreed with the traditional doctrine of preparation. The sinful Christian could neither regenerate himself through good works nor expect an infusion of unsought grace. "Instead of sitting down in sloth, as if he had nothing to do, no encouragement to labor for the meat that endureth to everlasting life," Stiles wrote. The repentant sinner

> ought to be up and doing, and work out his salvation with fear and trembling, knowing, that on his faithful improvement of the talents and advantages he enjoys, *it is God that worketh in him.* . . . [26] (My emphasis)

It was this convergence of opinion on the nature of the conversion process (a gradual one, discernible by its fruits) and on man's role in that process (an active one, whether through "Evangelical Humiliation," attendance on the "Means," study of the scriptures or, more commonly, all three) that paved the way for Stiles' formulation of the problem in his *Discourse on the Christian Union* and made that formulation truly reflective of a broad spectrum of opinion. "I suppose we are . . . agreed in the consequences and connexions of these two principles," Stiles wrote,

> the one governing a holy life, and exemplifying or rather diversifying itself in all the graces and ornaments of the moral behavior; the other in our justification, or entitling us, not by way of merit, but according to the constitution of grace, to all the benefits of the mediatorial atonement . . . There are indeed some different apprehensions among us on this subject. We all agree that Christ is the great propitiation: we do not place propitiation in faith or good works. The only question then is, what is the condition and appointed term in us, which entitled us to the benefits and fruits of Christ's righteousness? It is agreed on all hands, (that) whatever it is, it is not however meritorious; nor is the connexion between

> this term and receiving atonement so necessary as to preclude the sovereignty of grace.[27]

III

Writing sixteen years before Stiles' conciliation pamphlet appeared, the Reverend Experience Mayhew thought he saw a bedrock of agreement underlying the disputes over regeneration and election. "I conceive some Grounds to hope," he wrote in 1744,

> for a better Accommodation of some of the Points in Controversy, betwixt those who are commonly called Calvinists, and such as are called Arminians.

Moreover, Mayhew thought this reconciliation might be affected "without the least Damage to the Substance of that Hypothesis which Calvinists endeavour to support, against those who are for the Arminian Scheme . . . "[28] The book is important because it suggests that a sentiment for theological reconciliation existed during the Awakening, but also and more importantly, because the points upon which Mayhew thought some agreement existed were precisely the points upon which Ezra Stiles, writing in 1761, asserted that agreement had in fact appeared.

Mayhew began with the assertion that both Calvinists and Arminians were "fully of Opinion" that "no Man can perform any good Action (meaning by good what is in a proper and strict Sense so) 'till after he is born of the Spirit, or created anew into good Works." He called this a "natural Impotence" and illustrated it with a string of Biblical metaphors: a blind man cannot see, a deaf man cannot hear, a "Thorn-Bush" cannot bear figs, a "Bramble-Bush" cannot bear grapes. But there is "another Kind of Impotency," Mayhew asserted, "which arises only from Error in Men's Judgement, and Obstinacy in their Wills." This second kind of "Cannot" or "moral Impotency" could be cured by good Instructions and Arguments." By such "reasoning" and good Instructions men could learn to subdue the "Obstinacy in their Wills," and acknowledge the following truths: 1) their inherent sinfulness; 2) their inherent inability to satisfy the demands of the Covenant; 3) their consequent need of regenerating grace; and 4) their belief in and reliance on the "Good Tidings" of Jesus Christ as mediator of their sins. In this Mayhew thought that unregenerate sinners might "seek and obtain" saving grave without relying on the merits of their own virtue, "they having Nothing to recommend them to Him, or to plead with Him, but their own Poverty and Misery, and the Riches of this Grace and Mercy, and His most gracious Covenant."[29]

The Arminian dissent from Calvinist orthodoxy was not based on a rejection of the idea of innate depravity, as we have seen. Nor did the Arminians reject the necessity of regeneration; nor did they assert that men could achieve salvation by virtue of good works. What they did object to was the Calvinist image of an angry and vengeful God and the corollary idea that men had no role to play in the regeneration process.

But as Perry Miller has shown, these objections had been fully accepted by the founding generation and articulated in their Covenant, or Federal Theology.[30]   From this perspective Mayhew's solution was thoroughly orthodox as far as New England Calvinism was concerned. It was also a politic one as far as the controversies of the 1740s and 1750s were concerned. In the first place, Mayhew retained both the notion of innate depravity *and* the idea of a loving and forgiving God: " . . . let the Dissenters from the Calvinian Doctrines be told," he suggested,

> that the Doctrine of original Sin is indeed a great Truth . . . but that it is true also, that God had a Design of glorifying His Grace and Mercy, in the Redemption of Mankind when fallen into a State of Sin . . . [31]

Mayhew thought that "If these Truths are owned and allowed . . . many People would not be so averse to the Doctrine of original sin as they now seem to be."

In the second place, with regard to the Doctrine of Election, Mayhew gave man an active role to play (Preparation) while denying that men could earn their own salvation through good works. "We must not stay [passive] 'till we are renewed and sanctified by the Spirit," he explained, "but out of a Sense of our Misery, make Haste to Christ to do it for us."

> Tho' we cannot regenerate our selves, yet it is not true, that we cannot apply our selves to Christ to work this great Change in us by his Spirit. And he invites and requires us thus to do.[32]

"Let this Doctrine be owned and preached among us," Mayhew suggested, "and it is possible Arminians may then think that they have far less to cavil against in our Doctrine of Regeneration, than they should have if this were denied."[33]

Although Mayhew's resolution of the disagreements revealed by the Great Awakening took a step toward an acceptable compromise, it left a great deal to be desired. As far as the Separatists and the more rigid of the Calvinists were concerned it impugned the sovereignty of God and it left unresolved the problem of whether the sacraments themselves were to be regarded as a means of preparation or an emblem of election. As far as the Arminians were concerned, it left unresolved the role of attendance on the means and cognitive knowledge in the preparation process. Nevertheless, it did offer grounds for agreement on the more central issues of innate depravity and the obligation of sinners in the regeneration process. And it did, in the estimation of at least one recent historian, become "commonly accepted" among all but the most insistent of both parties.[34]

Thus, Ezra Stiles, sixteen years later, could confidently assert that,

> I find that both reputed Calvinists and Arminians, especially of the clergy, agree in admitting the depravity of human nature in all its powers and affections – the absolute inability to faith and holiness without the special influences, assistances and operations of the spirit on the human mind over and above the eluciated and inspired discoveries of those already revealed – that to his enlightening energies is to be attributed the principle of regeneration – that we are justified in the sight of God, not for good works, but alone for the sake of Christ and his atonement tho' they may differ in defining the nature of atonement, yet all agree in making it the sole foundation of justification – that the benefits of Christ's righteousness are appropriated to believers by *faith*, as the condition of our receiving the atonement.[35]

Mayhew's book had indeed, as he had hoped it would, "serve(d) to quiet the tumultuating Thoughts" of both Arminians and Calvinists, if only temporarily.[36]

I do not mean to argue that evangelical Calvinism and Arminianism had thoroughly reconciled their doctrinal differences and adopted a common theology. Obviously they had not. Piety and formalism had from the beginning of New England's history threatened to tear apart the Puritan synthesis. And they eventually did so; in the nineteenth-century Old Calvinism survived as but a remnant, totally unable to contain the forces of evangelicalism on the one hand and liberalism on the other.

What I do want to argue is that, between the ebbing of the Great Awakening in the mid-1740s and the American Revolution, this growing apart was temporarily arrested, or at least obscured, by a counter-movement of attempted reintegration; that this movement of resynthesis grew out of the apprehensions both sides felt when brought by the contentions and disputes of the Awakening to the very edge of the gulf that had grown between them. This movement toward reconciliation was led by a group of congregational clergymen, called Old Calvinists, who had aligned themselves with neither side during the early 1740s. The Old Calvinist movement, seeking as it did to restore the apparent unity of the founding generation, was an important source of that hope of redemption that we have recently come to see underlying the Revolutionary movement of the 1770s. The present chapter has shown how Evangelical Calvinists and Arminians had come to roughly similar understandings of the problems most central to New England's theological tradition — the nature of man and the nature of the regeneration process. The next chapter describes a similar convergence of opinion on the ecclesiastical problems that had been revealed by the Great Awakening.

Old Calvinist Ecclesiastical Thought

The Old Calvinists, as we have seen, were pleased with the revival of religious interest that accompanied the Great Awakening. Unlike the Old Lights, they looked upon the manifestation of piety as a work of God, opened their pulpits to George Whitefield, sought to give advice and counsel to the newly awakened in their congregations, and hoped for a continuation of this "great and merciful Revival of Religion." Rather than trying to squash the revivals, as the Old Lights attempted to do, they sought to incorporate its piety into New England's established religious forms.[1]

To do this required that Old Calvinists condemn what they saw as the excesses of the Awakening, particularly its antinomian and separatist impulses. But their desire to incorporate the piety of the Awakening required that they do more than criticize; they also had to purposefully and creatively address the ecclesiastical problems raised by the revivals. The most pressing of these concerned, first, the qualifications necessary for admission to church membership and the sacraments and, secondly, the authority of ministers and laity within individual congregations.

In attempting to resolve these problems the Old Calvinists returned to the vision and rhetoric enunciated by the Cambridge Platform of 1648. But this turned out to be an ironic traditionism, for when set in the context of Post-Awakening Congregationalism, the principles of the Cambridge Platform revealed a latent modernism that would have startled their seventeenth-century formulators. Out of the Old Calvinists' attempt to incorporate the piety of the Awakening into existing religious forms there gradually emerged a body of ecclesiastical thought whose essence was best expressed not in the Cambridge Platform of 1648 but in a new appreciation of theological pluralism.

I

Antinomianism had long threatened to undo New England Puritanism. The crisis created by Anne Hutchinson and her followers in the very first decade of settlement had early revealed the fragility of the Puritan synthesis of piety and formalism. Throughout the colonial period the spiritism of the brethren had periodically burst through the confines of Puritan orthodoxy.

The Old Calvinists responded to the antinomianism of the Great Awakening by reemphasizing, as we have seen, the complexity of the conversion process. Conviction of one's sinful state, no matter how startling and moving an experience, was only one in a series of steps leading to complete regeneration. A truly holy conversion could be validated only by sanctification, i.e., the display of steady and consistent religious practice. "True Conversion," William Hart explained in 1742,

> supposes that in consequence of this renovation of the tempers of our minds [i.e., conviction of one's sinful nature], there does follow, a thorou' Reformation of our Lives, and a regular, habitual practise of all the Virtues of the Christian life, in the course of a religious, righteous and blameless conversation. And when this is wanting; there is certainly, no true conversion, whatever secret and high experiences and testimonies of the spirit, that they are the children of God, such Persons may pretend to.[2]

This was a relatively uncontested position, one that even Jonathan Edwards, that champion of affectionate religion, espoused.

The problem of separatism was more difficult. The founding generation had gone to great lengths to deny that their flight across the Atlantic had been an act of separation, and their writings could be and were used to condemn the separations of the 1740s and 1750s. But the rise of Liberal Religion greatly complicated the matter for the Old Calvinists. Their commitment to inherited orthodoxy would not allow them to simply condemn all separations and thereby give tacit endorsement to the latitudinarianism of many of their liberal colleagues. As with the problem of conversion experiences, the Old Calvinists had to distinguish between valid and invalid separations.

No one thought this problem through more carefully than David McGregore, an Irish immigrant settled as pastor of the church at Londonderry, New Hampshire. In 1741 McGregore had given his support to the Awakening but had urged that conversion experiences be carefully gauged against the standards enunciated in scripture. "Blessed be God, that we have our Bibles."[3] In the aftermath of the Awakening he addressed himself to the problem of separations.

On the one hand, McGregore was appalled by the separations that had rent the fabric of New England Congregationalism. "What is the reason," he asked, "why Christianity makes so little progress in the world . . . ?" The reason, or at least "one main reason," was "the bitter party spirit, the fierce tempers, the anti-christian lives of many of its professors."

> 'Tis an observation which has been often made, and which is a sad truth, that the greatest evils which have befallen christian societies, are those which flow from intestine divisions, growing upon the decay of love.[4]

The Awakening that he had previously endorsed as "a work of God" had somehow left New England Puritanism "not only divided, but subdivided, crumbled almost into atoms of parties." Where he had previously urged caution, he now urged magnanimity and forbearance, warning his readers to "beware of party names" and not to be "forward in condemning one another as heretics": in a word, to avoid those things which "tend to irritate and inflame men's spirits and by this means to widen divisions." "Be on your guard against a separating spirit," he warned. "This is an anti-christian spirit."[5]

Had McGregore left the matter at this juncture his work would not have been significant. The call for tolerance, after all, came most easily from those most utterly and completely opposed to the Awakening. What makes McGregore's work different is his attempt to distinguish between valid and invalid separations. "I would by no means," he wrote in 1765, "have any thing that I have said, be so understood, as if I condemned all separations: Some are no doubt lawful, and [a] matter of duty." He then specified the conditions that he thought justified separation: preaching a doctrine of works; omitting to preach on the necessity of justification and of regeneration by faith; deriding or denying the extraordinary influences and operations of the Holy Spirit; or "if a professsing church is gone off from the Gospel of Christ, to another Gospel." Those separations were invalid, on the other hand, which sprang from a minister's lack of zeal and evangelical piety. McGregore compared separations begun on these latter grounds to the actions of the Donatists of the fourth century. Their crime was not a doctrinal one, but the crime of schism.

> The church was too corrupt for them to abide in her fellowship: They pretended to set up pure churches. By their uncharitable breaches of communion, they rent to pieces the seamless coat of our Lord.

In other words, separations arising from extra-doctrinal complaints, i.e., from the desire for spiritual purity, "are separations to which heaven will not give its sanction."[6]

By thus identifying the essentials of Calvinist theology, much as Stiles and the other Old Calvinists had done before him, and by erecting a protective dike around all churches in which such principles were professed, McGregore hoped to remedy what he called "the ecclesiastical anarchy of this day." Not that he thought his proposals alone would be sufficient; he rather hoped that they "might dispose ministers and other christians to enter into a serious enquiry,"

> whether a common fence about the churches, might not be likely to prevent many of these bad things, and to keep out the boar of the forest, from entering in to waste the vineyard at his pleasure.[7]

Others of the Old Calvinists made similar suggestions to arrest the wave of separations that were rending apart their churches. In 1751 Solomon Williams, pastor of the church at Lebanon, Connecticut, published a book entitled *The Sad Tendency of Divisions and Contentions in the Churches.* . . . Williams had never seen, he said, a time when the churches were "so divided and distracted, as the present. . . ." He felt obliged to warn his readers that if the "divisions and contentions in [the] churches" were "continued in," they would "bring on their Ruin and Desolation." And like McGregore, he saw the solution to lie in "an harty union in all [the] things necessary to salvation," by which he meant the basic Calvinist doctrines of inherent sinfulness, atonement, and regeneration through unmerited grace. If Calvinists of all persuasions could "be united in, and joined together in the same mind and judgment" on these essential doctrines, then "all other concerns would run into this great one, like Rivers into the Sea, which would swallow up all." Williams believed that recognition of the doctrines they held in common would "most effectually teach you not to separate any interest, design or desire of yours, from God's interest, and Christ's Kingdom."[8]

Williams and McGregore were correct, of course: Separatists and the churches from which they detached themselves *did* share a bedrock of common theological assumptions. And they *were* the assumptions outlined by Williams and McGregore. But it was this very fact that rendered their work ineffectual, for the great bulk of separations arose not over matters of theology but over questions of church discipline and admission to the sacraments. "They profess well," one Separatist explained of the congregation he had left,

> but they are corrupt in practice, in admission of members, opening the door too wide, letting in even all sorts of persons, without giving any evidence at all of their faith in Christ and repentance toward God.[9]

None of the Separatists criticized the practices of the established churches more thoroughly or more searchingly than Jonathan Edwards.

"I know the danger of corrupt principles," he declared in 1750. Liberal theological ideas and loose ecclesiastical practices had seeped into every corner and cranny of the land, threatening the debasement of federal theology and the pollution of New England churches.[10]

The most dangerous of these tendencies—"the great thing which I have scrupled"—was the dead formalism that had come to characterize the owning of the covenant. Persons desiring admission to communion simply recited a stereotyped conversion experience, or sometimes a mere profession of belief that made no pretense of a work of God in their souls. Owning the covenant had become so formal and meaningless as to be hardly distinguishable from the Anglican recitation of creeds. New Englanders typically neglected their spiritual state and religious duties until they married and then suddenly petitioned for admission to the church in order to have their children baptized. As a result,

> God's own children and true disciples of Christ are obliged to receive those as their *brethren*, admit them to the *communion of saints*, and embrace them in the highest acts of Christian society, even in their great *feast of love*, where they feed together on the body and blood of Christ, whom yet they have no reason to look upon otherwise than as *enemies of the cross of Christ*, and haters of their heavenly Father and dear Redeemer.[11]

These are, undeniably, the sentiments and objections of a Separatist: the failure of church discipline, the corruption of the Sacraments by contact with the unregenerate, the designation of the ungracious as enemies of Christ, and the personal odiousness of attending communion with them.[12]

That Edwards was sensitive to the charge of separatism can be seen in his nearly-frantic denials, repeated over and again. In *Distinguishing Marks*, in *Observations and Reflections on Mr. Brainerd's Life*, and in *Treatise on Religious Affections*, he castigated the Separatists as "wild people" possessed by a "lunatic" spirit. In *Humble Inquiry*, he took special pains to disassociate himself from these fanatics. One thing above all others, he said, had caused him "to go about this business with so much backwardness":

> the fear of a bad improvement some ill-minded people might be ready, at this day, to make of the doctrine here defended, particularly that wild, enthusiastical sort of people, who have of late gone into unjustifiable separations, even renouncing the ministers and churches of the land in general, under pretence of setting up a pure church.[13]

Edwards insisted that he meant not to gather the saints out of the world, but to inject piety into the churches. But this could hardly disguise the Separatist-like longing for a communion of the saints that throbbed just beneath its surface. The more he wrote, the more clearly he revealed himself.

In *Humble Inquiry*, Edwards sought to justify his restriction of communion to visible saints. By "visible saints" he meant "such as are in profession and in the eye of the church's Christian judgment, Godly or gracious persons." This was a carefully drawn and judicious formulation. On the one hand, Edwards knew that even under the eye of Christian judgment, grace remained an elusive thing, hidden from public inspection and examination. "These things have all their existence in the soul, which is out of our neighbors' view." What he wanted the churches to insist upon was not grace itself but sanctification, the visible presence of grace in outward behavior.

> The question is not, whether Christ has made converting grace or piety itself the condition or rule of His people's admitting any to the priviledges of members in full communion with them . . . [but] the credible profession and visibility of these things, that is the church's rule in this case . . . It is a visibility to the eye of a Christian judgment.[14]

On the other hand, he insisted that the churches require more than a profession of belief. "It is not visibility of moral sincerity only, but a visibility of circumcision of heart, or saving conversion, that is necessary." The argument that moral sincerity could qualify one for communion evaded the real issue, he charged, because moral sincerity made no pretense to saving grace. Moreover, in contrast to the persistence of the saints, moral sincerity was as liable to fade away "as the early dew and the morning cloud."

> If men do not pretend to have any oil in their vessels, what cause can there be to trust that their lamps will not go out? If they do not pretend to have any root in them, what cause is there for any disappointment when they wither away?[15]

Richard Mather's generation would have found little in Edwards' treatise to complain of; the problem with *Humble Inquiry* was not that it demanded a departure from orthodox Calvinism, but a return to it. To have insisted upon public relation and congregational approbation as terms for communion in 1749 was to betray a fatal naivete. In *Humble Inquiry*, Edwards revealed the extent to which his mind had denied its own experience in order to feed, undisturbed, upon the decaying ideas of the past. By 1751 Edwards had so abandoned himself to his vision of a pure church that he had lost the ability to distinguish the requirements of the institution from the desires of the saints.

Thus he admitted, at the very end of this long treatise, that the experience with public relations during the Awakening had been "enough to put all sober and judicious people forever out of conceit of it." The practice had generated spiritual pride in the Children of God and, worse still, had led even sincere Christians to mistake the images flickering across their imaginations for divine communications. Churches had been torn asunder and the established order undermined. Here, in one page, expressed in Edwards' own clear and forceful prose, were the unavoidable, irrepressible lessons of a decade, the lessons of the Great Awakening itself. Yet—the importance of this cannot be overemphasized—Edwards dismissed them in a single sentence: perhaps, he suggested, relations of conversion experiences could be conducted "under some public regulation, and under the direction of skilful guides." Perry Miller's response to Cotton Mather's role in the witch trials is apt here: we avert our gaze while, he, after admitting this single concession to reality, flees up the ladder of orthodoxy and soothes himself with fresh dreams of the communion of saints.[16]

II

The moderates chose Solomon Williams of Lebanon to write their response to Edwards. His book, *The True State of the Question*, did not appear until two years after Edwards' *Humble Inquiry* had appeared, by which time Edwards had been dismissed and the controversy had largely subdued. Most historians have regarded *True State* as a rather weak reply. Edwards' *Humble Inquiry* is clear, forceful, incisive, persuasive, even devastating; Williams' *True State* is crabbed, humorless, shrill, brittle, unconvincing and barely able to contain the contradictions it claims to harmonize. Perry Miller thus concludes that Edwards ran Williams through a meat-grinder. But this misses the point. Edwards was able to display such brutally consistent logic only because he had abandoned the dualism of the past, the dualism that had always underlay non-separating congregationalism. Conversely, the significance of *True State* lies not in the failure of its logic or the febrility of its arguments, but in its attempt to maintain that traditional dualism.

Williams began by assuring his readers that the issue between Edwards and him was not one of doctrine but application. He had no controversy with Edwards over the absolute necessity of free grace, the inefficacy of good works, and all the related points of Calvinist dogma. Also like Edwards, he believed that in admitting persons to full communion the church ought to look for signs of an inward condition. It was not "the visibility of moral sincerity, but the moral evidence of gospel sincerity" which should be the basis of judgment. The question was not whether communion ought to be restricted to the graceful—"since 'tis allowed on all hands that the church ought to admit none but visible saints"—but how such sainthood should and could be verified. "I conceive," Williams wrote,

> that the whole argument, and indeed the whole controversy, turns upon this single point, viz., what is that evidence which, by divine appointment, the church is to have of the saintship of those who are admitted to the outward priviledges of the convenant of grace?[17]

The question was not one of doctrine but of how to apply the doctrine, how to verify election. That problem had always been the conundrum of American Puritanism. Edwards' insistence that election could only be verified by public relation struck Williams as sadly out of touch with recent experience. "One would think that the late dreadful consequences of such sort of doings in this land had been enough to convince every judicious Christian of the sinfulness of it." Similarly, Edwards' suggestion that "skillful guides" be employed to lend regularity to public relations seemed to Williams an artificial solution, likely to produce only standardized relations and hypocritical communicants. "Whether this is like to promote the Honour of God, or be a scandal and reproach to his name, seems not very difficult to determine."[18]

Edwards' insistence upon public relations promised not only to scandalize God, but to destroy His churches in New England. During the 1750s the moderates found themselves pressed between Anglicanism on the one hand and Separatism on the other. Edwards' proposal threatened to turn the screws of that vise even more tightly, squeezing the remaining communicants out of the established churches. For if sincere Christians should find themselves excluded from their own churches because of overly rigid requirements for communion, they would surely go elsewhere. And Williams knew where they would go: to "the Church of England and all [the] Arminian churches." The orthodox churches, meanwhile, by establishing ever more rigid communion requirements, "will fall into Independency, Antinomian separations, and crumble into as many separate churches as they have different methods of determining men's conversions." Far from revivifying the established churches, Edwards' proposal only promised to rush them into destruction. This view was widespread among the moderates. John Devotion of Saybrook, Chauncy Whittelsey of New Haven, and others responded to Edwards by publicly venting the same fear.[19]

Williams' solution was to accept profession of belief and submission to Christ as emblematic of grace and therefore sufficient for admission to communion. Moral sincerity was insufficient in and of itself, but should be accepted *as an indication* of inward grace. Williams put it this way:

> The outward duties of morality and worship, when to appearance they are sincerely performed, are by the church in their publick judgment to be charitably thought to be the product of the great inward duties of love of God, and acceptance of Christ. The latter ought not only to be pretended to, but exhibited by the former . . . and this visibility must be such as to a judgment of rational charity, makes them appear as real saints.[20]

The difference between Edwards and Williams was thus etched clearly and sharply. Edwards, tottering on the brink of separatism, pleaded his vision of a pure church, in which the saints could feed upon their mystical dinner undisturbed by the presence of natural men. Williams, on the other hand, defended a system whose distinctive quality had always been its attempt to bring most men into the church.

Both of these understandings differed substantially from the Arminian position, which was most succinctly put forth by Charles Chauncy in his *Breaking of Bread . . .* (Boston, 1772). The central point of difference lay in Chauncy's contention that the sacraments were a means of conversion rather than an emblem of holiness. "It is by the use of this divinely appointed mean[s] of grace," Chauncy wrote, "that we are to grow, from the state of babes and children, to that of complete men in Christ."[21]

Given this understanding, Chauncy was far more liberal in admitting persons to communion. He thought the Eucharist "admirably well adapted to promote the edification of *all* that come to it in the serious exercise of faith, though their faith, at present, should not be such as will argue their being 'born from above.'" But this is not to imply that Chauncy was willing to admit anyone to communion. He specifically disbarred not only "the securely wicked," the "vicious and ungodly," and all who "love the ways of sin," but as well those who feel "the bonds of God," in only "a low feeble degree, so as they have no power to form their temper, or thoroughly touch their conscience." Those he would admit to communion included all whose "turn of mind is serious and considerate" and perform the external obligations of Christians, and, most especially, "the fearful and scrupulous, those who labor of doubts and have their minds perplexed with [religious] difficulties."[22]

What Chauncy had done was to deny the special status and character of the sacraments. Attendance upon the preaching of the word, prayer, study of the scriptures, baptism and communion were to be "regarded without distinction, or discrimination." In terms of ecclesiastical practice, though not in terms of theology, Chauncy and the Arminians had thus abandoned the distinction between saints and sinners, and with it the perplexing problem of distinguishing between them.[23]

The Old Calvinist position thus stood midway between the evangelical demand for a relation of conversion and the Arminian practice of admitting to communion those who made no pretense at all of saving grace. No satisfactory resolution seemed possible, though innumerable tracts appeared on all sides of the question during the 1750s. Not until the end of the decade were the Old Calvinists able to see the outlines of a compromise that would, they hoped, put an end to controversy and stabilize New England's fragile ecclesiastical constitution.

III

The precipitating event occurred in the summer of 1758 when the church at Wallingford, Connecticut invited James Dana to become its pastor. A minority of the congregation opposed Dana's appointment and appealed to the New Haven Consociation to block his installation. When Dana was installed over the Consociation's opposition a furious dispute erupted over the balance of power between individual churches and regional structures of authority like the New Haven Consociation. The fact that most of these consociations had fallen into the hands of the New Lights has led several historians to assume that the opposition to their authority came from the Old Lights and that it was narrowly political in origin and character.[24] In fact, the leading voices in the dispute were Old Calvinist and reflected a recognition on their part that the organization of New England's religious life was no longer adequate to the exigencies of the post-Awakening period. "We are breaking to pieces in our churches very fast," was the way one Old Calvinist put it.[25] The manifold disputes over admission to communion and the settling of new ministers, as Noah Hobart explained in 1759, "put people on inquiring into the nature of ecclesiastical councils . . . and the authority they have. . . ."[26] None were more forward in this reexamination than the Old Calvinists William Hart and Ezra Stiles.

William Hart, minister of the church at Saybrook, was by nature inclined to avoid controversy. He once told his friend Ezra Stiles that "a party spirit will always do too little one way and too much the other."[27] His attitude toward "matters of doubtful disputation" was to advise that they "be left undetermined" rather than cause "any breach of charity [or] alienation of affection. . . ."[28] He portrayed the disputes over admission to the sacraments by way of the following parable:

> The father of the whole family of his grace furnishes excellent tea and loaf sugar for his whole family, leaving it to them to provide dishes. All receive their tea with praise and thanksgiving; but one company chooses to drink it out of wooden dishes, another out of peuter, another silver, another china. Shall they on this account reproach each other as aliens or bastards? . . . no, by no means.[29]

This attitude left him temperamentally ill-disposed toward Connecticut's Saybrook Platform of 1708, which had given regional consociations a great deal of authority in settling ecclesiastical disputes. The Wallingford controversy suggested to him that in the context of the religious diversity of the 1750s such regional structures of authority did as much to intensify disputes as they did to resolve them. In the aftermath of the controversy at Wallingford, Hart suggested that the consociations be stripped of their power to impose a settlement and that their decisions be only advisory. He contended that if consociations were "founded on, and [arose] out of the mutual agreements of several single pastors and churches," and that if they were given "no other than an advisory authority," the various disputes over admission to communion and settlement of new ministers "may easily be settled . . . on congregational principles. . . . "[30]

A career of mediating ecclesiastical disputes[31] had brought Ezra Stiles, minister of the Second Congregational church at Newport, to the same conclusion. In his *Discourse on the Christian Union*, delivered the same year Hart published his analysis, Stiles subjected the performance of regional ecclesiastical structures to a lengthy and searching examination. His conclusion was that the diversity of religious denominations and sects in New England had rendered the work of such structures "fruitless and to little purpose, besides a temporary embroiling of the churches." The "notion of erecting the polity of either [New Lights or Old Lights] into universal dominion to the destruction of the rest," he condemned as "but an airy vision [that] may serve to inflame a temporary enthusiasm, but can never succede." The authority of extra-congregational structures should be "advisory only" for, "strictly speaking, congregational councils have no power at all."[32]

What makes Stiles' *Discourse on the Christian Union* significant, however, is the fact that he took his analysis one step further than did Hart, to suggest that the diversity of religious forms might be a positive good, that the great variety of New England's denominations and sects might be balanced against one another in such a way as to create, of themselves, a new stability. "Providence," he explained,

> has planted the British Americas with a variety of sects, which will unavoidably become a mutual balance upon one another . . . union may subsist in these

distinctions. . . . [for] the sects cannot destroy one another: all attempts this way will be fruitless — they may affect a temporary disturbance, but cannot produce a dissolution [for] each one subserves the mutual security of all.[33]

"Our grand security," Stiles later explained to Hart,

is in the multitude of sects and the public liberty necessary for them to cohabit together. In consequence of which the aggrieved of any communion will either pass over to another, or rise into new Sects and spontaneous societies. This and this only will learn us wisdom not to persecute one another.[34]

The Old Calvinist response to the ecclesiastical disputes of the post-Awakening period was thus to call upon New England's tradition of Congregational autonomy. Over and over again Stiles, Hart, Williams and others of the Old Calvinists invoked the authority of the founding generation and the ideals expressed by them in the Cambridge Platform of 1648. But this was an ironic traditionalism, for the formulators of the Cambridge Platform had drafted that document as a bulwark against exactly the sort of variety the Old Calvinists now called upon it to validate. That Ezra Stiles recognized the irony involved can be seen in his admission that while "union may subsist in these distinctions, coalescence [can subsist] only on the sameness of public sentiment which . . . has been effected in past ages, but can never be effected again . . . so great an alteration is made among mankind by science and letters."[35]

The Context of Religious Moderation:

Part II

Ministerial Associations
and Clerical Unity

In eighteenth-century New England ecclesiastical power lay with the individual congregations and with the councils and consociations that they controlled. Ministerial associations were unable to determine ecclesiastical affairs because they lacked constitutional legitimacy and because laymen were often suspicious of ministerial intentions. As Ebenezer Parkman of Westborough explained, "when what [is] to be done [is] of common and general concernment to ye chhs, this is not so undertaken by ministers themselves, but must be done as synods of councils, wherein it is needful to have ye brethren of ye chhs, that is, delegates to represent them."[1]

Ministerial associations suffered irregular attendance and rarely survived for more than fifteen or twenty years. Yet, feckless and evanescent as they were, they continued to proliferate during the course of the eighteenth century. As early as 1719 Benjamin Colman reported that "the ministers of every Vicinity here form themselves into Associations and have their stated meetings. . . . "[2] By 1740 ministerial associations existed in most regions of Massachusetts and in every county in Connecticut.[3]

These associations were formed and reformed "not as some doe imagine and pretend, to betray ye liberties of ye Chhs,"[4] but to provide isolated clergymen with emotional sustenance and intellectual stimulation, to help them deal with the day-to-day problems of parish life, and to maintain a rough consensus on theological and ecclesiastical problems. Ministerial associations were communal-like gatherings rather than political institutions; they celebrated fraternal relations rather than ecclesiastical power. Most important, they provided the personal ligaments that bound the ministry together and enabled it to transcend issues that would otherwise have torn it apart. They provided, in a very real sense, the tie that binds. This will be apparent if we examine what actually happened when ministers gathered together, as Parkman said, "to assist, comfort and strengthen one another."[5] The following pages will discuss: 1) the way in which ministerial associations grew out of and reflected an underlying web of personal and familial relations; 2) the way association meetings were actually conducted; 3) the services they performed for the larger community; 4) their attempts to clarify the role of ministers generally; 5) the way in which they fashioned a consensus on theological and ecclesiastical questions; 6) their role in church discipline; and, finally, 7) the more personal ways they found to bind ministers to one another, or, as Joseph Baxter put it, to "give them onenesse of heart."[6]

I

The composition of ministerial associations often reflected an underlying web of personal and familial relationships. As J.W.T. Youngs has pointed out, most New England ministers settled in the area in which they had grown up. For example, of the twenty-two clergymen settled in Boston between 1690 and 1740, seventeen had been raised within ten miles of the metropolis.[7] The same was true of other areas. This meant that the regional ministerial associations were often composed of men who shared the perceptions and experiences common to those who grew up in a particular area. Consider the example of the Bradford Association in Essex County. Of the twenty ministers who joined the Association during its existence (1719-1740), sixteen had been born and raised in Essex County.[8] Moreover, of the four "outsiders," two—Joseph Parsons and Samuel Bacheller—had moved to and established roots in Essex County well before their call to Essex County pulpits (Bacheller married a Haverhill woman and joined the Rowley First Church in 1728, seven years before his settlement at the Haverhill Third Church in 1735; Joseph Parsons was keeping the Exeter school and attending the Salisbury church when he was called to the Bradford pulpit in 1726.)[9] Thus, of the twenty Bradford Association clergymen, only two, John Brown of Haverhill First and John Tufts of Newbury Second, were new to Essex County when they settled there as ministers.

Common origins were complemented by family relationships. Again, the Bradford Association illustrates the point: nearly half of the Association members (nine out of twenty) were related to one another by ties of blood, marriage, or adoption. James Chandler of Georgetown was related to Moses Hale of Byfield by marriage and to John Chandler of Haverhill by virtue of having adopted his daughter. William Johnson of Newbury Fourth Church read theology with John Tufts of Newbury

Second Church (as did Abner Bayley of Salem, New Hampshire, First Church) and then married his sister-in-law; John Barnard of Andover was related to John Tucker of Newbury First by marriage.   John Chandler of Boxford Second Church and James Cushing of Haverhill Second were brothers, as were John Barnard of Andover North and Thomas Barnard of West Newbury First.   Ministerial associations thus grew out of, and were in turn colored by, deeply lying, permanent relationships between their members.   They must be thought of as part of the complex network of familial relations that bound together colonial communities and regions, rather than as modern professional organizations.

The organization and conduct of the meetings suggests that ministerial associations were less concerned with the exercise of power than with the enjoyments of fellowship.   Ebenezer Parkman said that his colleagues in the Marlborough Association spent their meetings talking, praying and singing together.   This was true of the other associations as well.   The Hampshire ministers, as one of them explained, "pray with one another and sing . . . every morning and evening. . . ."[10]   Ministerial meetings were a way for clergymen, as the Sherburne ministers said, to "unite our hearts and knitt them together."[11]

It is difficult to overemphasize the importance of this fraternal communion, for it was one of the central features of the associations. The ministry was a difficult and oftentimes disappointing work, a weariness to the flesh, as the ministers repeated over and again.   Above all else, the association meetings provided a change from the routine of rural agricultural life and a chance for ministers to buoy up one another's spirits, an opportunity, as one of the Sherburne ministers said, "to quicken and unite one another to diligence and fidelity in their work."[12]

In 1700 only six ministers were regularly settled on Massachusetts' eastern frontier; forty years later there were forty-two.   As the eighteenth century wore on a larger and larger percentage of the ministry served in remote and isolated townships.   Ministerial associations promised, first and more importantly, a chance for ministers to come out of the woods and fields to enjoy one another's company; it was a way, as Samuel Willard explained in 1704, to ameliorate "the inconveniences of him that is alone."[13]

Praying, singing and talking together were ways the associations did that; establishing a lending library was another.   In October of 1732 the Hampshire Association resolved to establish "a library for the use of the ministry in said county."   By the following April it had collected over one hundred and eighty pounds for that purpose. The Hampshire Association Library was furnished with "a complete catalogue," "a convenient wooden box" for transporting books, and a set of sixteen rules "for the government of the said library." Ministers attached great importance to the library. The minimum subscription was ten pounds, and nearly half of them gave twice that amount. Ten pounds represented about a tenth of an average minister's yearly salary.[14] Some had difficulty raising that much money. Next to William Williams' name in the Hampshire Association records appears this note: "to be paid the next Spring and . . . the Spring following."[15]

The associations also provided an opportunity for ministers to learn from one another. As a member of the Sherburne Association explained, "by holding forth and communicating unto one another light and knowledge . . . [we] may be greatly serviceable to one another."[16] Each meeting set a question for the following meeting, which each pastor was to study and prepare for discussion. This practice was common to all the associations but the Hampshire Association's program was probably the most ambitious. The "Proposals for the Best improvement of our Time at Association," adopted at its meeting of 12 October 1742, committed the ministers to a rigorous program that included, at each meeting: two doctrinal questions to be discussed; a "sermon *ad clerum*"; and the stipulation "that each member shall have a particular text of Scripture given to him to explain."[17] The Sherburne Association's program was less detailed and rigorous but pointed in the same direction: they hoped by "friendly disputes and debates about things that are more dark and unintelligible than others are" to "grow and increase in knowledge." Similarly the Marlborough Association, at the meeting in June 1739, voted "that every member make and bring written collections of what remarkable occurs in his reading, studies and conversation, etc., from one time of Association to another, and communicate the same for our mutual emolument and advantage."[18]

By preaching to each other, and by "opening" passages of scripture, ministers helped one another not only with matters of doctrine but with problems of style as well. Ultimately, clergymen rested their status and respect upon personal authority; they were eager to wrap themselves in an aura of professional competence and ministerial dignity. "The Gospel-Minister," explained William Rand of Sunderland, had to display "an exemplary and circumspect behavior . . . in order to save himself from contempt."[19] The ministerial associations helped clergymen maintain this sense of personal authority by providing a forum wherein they could perfect their preaching style, practice interpreting difficult Biblical texts, and display a professional carriage and deportment. Israel Loring, minister of the Sudbury First Church and member of the Marlborough Association from 1725 until 1762, took "great care to guard against all levity and everything unbecoming my august office . . . particularly [when] in

Company with my Brethren in the ministry."[20] The Sherburne ministers thought they could be most helpful to each other "not by lauding and flattering and complimenting one another," but "by admonishing and reproving one another for what is amiss" for "they may see failings in one another easier than in themselves." In this way ministers could help one another avoid "that contempt which people are exceeding prone to throw upon them."[21] This is a recurrent theme that appears in the association records over and over again. Thus, on 18 October 1715, the Sherburne ministers returned to the problem of maintaining personal authority in front of their congregations. They concluded that

> In this way of associating together the pastors of the churches have opportunity to admonish and reprove one another . . . [for] though they preach divine doctrine, yet if their conversation be earthly and sensual they are more likely to harden sinners than to convert them. And how unbecoming and disgraceful are unholy ministers to their profession; what a scandal doe they give to the profession, and occasion to blaspheme their high and holy calling . . . And therefore, that means of recovering those that fall, even that of admonition and reprehension, are ministers to use towards one another when there is occasion for it. And when they frequently associate together there is opportunity for it.[22]

Similarly the Bradford Association ministers agreed, at their first meeting, to "admit into the Councils, reproofs and censures of the Brethren so Associated and Assembled."[23] Ministerial associations existed not to exercise ecclesiastical power as much as to maintain personal authority.

The associations not only provided an opportunity for social intercourse and a school for personal deportment, they also gave clergymen a chance to discuss the practical problems involved in their work. Thus the Sherburne Association devoted sessions to examining how the growth of formality might be checked; how parishioners in spiritual distress could be comforted and encouraged; how to compose "popular sermons, or sermons for a vulgar auditory";[24] how to deal with strife and contention in their congregations; and how family prayers could be encouraged. Similarly, the Hampshire Association turned its attention to problems like: "the best methods to be taken in order to peace and comfort on a death-bed";[25] the meaning of God's "Late Frowning Dispensations";[26] "whether it be lawful to eat blood";[27] whether a Christian may marry a heathen; and the like. The Cambridge Associ-ation pondered such questions as: whether a man might lawfully marry his sister; whether ministers had an obligation to visit the sick "in times of epidemical and contagious distempers";[28] what steps might be taken to spread Christianity among the Indians; under what conditions marriages might be lawfully annulled; and "whether any self-killing be lawful."[29]   Other associations also devoted a large number of their sessions to such practical problems.   In this the associations served neither as legislators nor tribunals, but simply as gatherings to which ministers could turn for counsel and advice.

Most of the problems discussed by the associations were practical; but not all, for God's ambassadors in New England worked in a vineyard beset with thorns and thistles. As the Sherburne ministers put it, God had called them to labour "amongst a proud, factious, censorious people, where the devil reigns exceedingly."[30]   Clergymen thus found themselves beset with problems of discipline, the more difficult of which they brought to the associations for discussion and advice.

Until the Great Awakening, no area of a clergyman's work was more filled with contention than that of church discipline.   Both the Cambridge and the Saybrook Platforms lodged the powers of church discipline with Ruling Elders.[31]   But this allowed a great deal of latitude and practice accordingly varied greatly in both colonies. The town of Lebanon, Connecticut, for example, supported two churches at mid-century, which followed two very different practices.   At the Second Church, Eleazar Wheelock followed a very authoritarian procedure. Wheelock himself received accusations against members of his church, sent out summonses to the accused and to witnesses, and, rather than having cases heard at the church by the ruling elders, heard all cases in his own home, before *ad hoc* panels, chosen by himself, as he put it, "to advise and assist me on the matter."[32]   Most sanctions imposed by Wheelock consisted of public admonitions and confessions, but even cases of excommunication were handled in this manner. Silas Woodworth, for example, was dismissed from the Second Church in July 1743 without having his case referred to the congregation (he had been convicted of "creeping under the eves of the [meeting] house in an unbecoming manner.")[33] This manner of proceeding generated a number of protests from members of Wheelock's congregation, but they seem to have been ineffectual.

At the Lebanon First Church, by way of contrast, Solomon Williams followed a more liberal course. Most cases he heard involved only confession and public admonition; these were handled by Williams and a regularly chosen church council.   But cases involving excommunication were heard first by Williams and the church council, then referred, without decision or comment, to the assembled congregation. In these latter cases the council confined itself to arranging the evidence on each side, so as to make the presentation to the congregation as orderly and clear as possible.[34]

This sharp contrast of procedure in a single town illustrates the lack of system or regularity of procedure that plagued the administration of church discipline throughout New England during the Colonial Period. Thomas Clap's description of the resulting chaos, offered in 1732, was probably an accurate one. "What renders the Administration of sacred Discipline yet the more difficult," he explained, "is that we have few or no stated and known Rules for a Minister's Direction. . . . "

> When any case comes upon the Board, the Rule seems to be, not to do what is just and right in itself, but what may happen to serve the present Turn. . . . Hence one ecclesiastical Judgment is no Precedent for another, and some Methods are not always observed in some cases, but Things left fluctuating in uncertainties.

Clap thought this lack of regular and stated procedures was a central cause of the "distempered Heats" that continually plagued colonial pastors. The lack of settled procedures "gives People occasion of quarrelling with one another, involves their Ministers in Difficulties, and exposes them to the odious Aspersions and Imputations of Partiality, Unsteadiness and the like." A regular, codified method of procedure, on the other hand, would strengthen and steady the administration of ecclesiastical discipline and thereby remove a chief source of trouble for the ministers. Clap thought this could be achieved by commissioning "some aged and experienced New England Divine" to collect the rules and procedures used in Scotland and France and make them available to the New England clergy. No such legislative sage appeared, of course; in his absence New England ecclesiastical affairs continued to be ruled by strife and contention. As a result, ministers often brought their most difficult cases to the regional associations for advice.[35]

The need for council and advice in matters of church discipline was thus another one of the motives that drew ministers together in associations. When the Bradford Association was formed at Thomas Symmes' home in Bradford on 3 June 1719, it agreed "to hear and consider any cases as shall be laid before us."[36] Similarly, the Marlborough Association ministers, at their initial meeting on 5 June 1725, agreed "to consider any case, that might be laid before them. . . . "[37] When the Hampshire Association was organized in October of 1731, it committed itself to discussing the problems of "due management of church discipline in our churches."[38]

A wide range of disciplinary cases were thus brought before the associations for their consideration and advice. Israel Loring of Sudbury asked the Marlborough Association, of which he was a member, to discuss several passages of Scripture "touching the proof of a person's being drunk."[39] At its October 1731 meeting the Hampshire Association discussed the case of "a man [who] hath humbled a virgin," and a second case in which two men had fought one another "for a considerable time, to the uttmost of their power" over possession of a church pew.[40] Other meetings examined cases of theft, fornication, lying, and the like.[41]

The associations also agreed to hear cases presented by ministers not formally members of their own gathering. At a meeting in 1740 the Bradford Association "voted, to hear cases of any who care to present them for advice to the Association." The Marlborough Association similarly agreed to hear cases brought to them "by any member, or other persons."[42] Thus, on 17 April 1723, the Rev. Daniel Putnam of North Reading, who had never before attended meetings of the Bradford Association, appeared before that body "for advice how to manage a controversy between some of his church members."[43] On 25 April 1725 the Rev. Samuel Ruggles of Billerica asked the Bradford Association how to handle "some cases of difficulty with his church."[44] On 28 October 1740 the Rev. Joseph Dorr of Mendon First Church ("who was occasionally with us") asked the Marlborough Association to advise him on a case of discipline within his church.[45] The following August the Association again advised Dorr and also Rev. Grindall Rawson of South Hadley on matters of discipline within their respective churches.[46]

Most of these matters were routine—helping individual ministers determine the proper sanctions to be employed against drunkeness, for example, or theft, fornication, fighting, or lying. But some were more difficult and these often consumed entire meetings. A case brought before the Plymouth Association on 8 April 1729 was resolved only "after a long debate."[47] When John Emerson of Topsfield and Oliver Peabody of the Indian church at Natick brought their cases before the Bradford Association in October of 1733, the assembled ministers consumed the entire day considering the problems involved and were not able to produce an "advice" until the following morning.[48]

Though the associations offered ministers advice in handling disciplinary cases, they did not attempt to *ajudicate* such cases. This is important for understanding the role of ministerial associations in ecclesiastical affairs. In the first place, the associations acted only when cases were brought to them; in no instance did an association pass judgment upon a case of church discipline without having been asked to do so by the minister involved. Secondly, when confronted with particularly controversial cases, the associations typically referred them to more duly constituted bodies, usually to ecclesiastical councils, sometimes to the particular congregation involved, still other times to the local courts. Thus the Bradford Association advised Daniel Putnam of Reading to present a particularly difficult case to his entire congregation for determination.[49]   When John Swift of Framingham presented a case of perjury to the Marlborough Association for advice, they suggested that he turn the problem over to the civil authorities, "rather than involve the church in debates. . . . "[50]

Thirdly, the associations oftentimes simply commiserated with an embroiled pastor or went out of their way to avoid becoming involved. The Bradford Association records for 17 June 1730 contain this note: "Discoursed of Mr. [Moses] Hale's difficulties by reason of a new meeting house set-up in his parish. Mr. Hale concluded with Prayer."[51] When Abner Bayley of North Metheun described a particularly contentious problem in his parish, the assembled ministers decided only to avoid meeting in Bayley's parish for a while.[52]

The role of ministerial associations was only to offer advice to distressed pastors, not to supervise church discipline, nor to ajudicate church disputes. The Hampshire Association made this point explicit at its meeting of 13 October 1741. "We are far from assuming to ourselves a power to call churches or particular persons to an account, and Pretend to no more in our Associations, than to give the Best Judgment and Advice we can. . . . We are not a judicatory. . . . "[53] As Joseph Baxter of Mendon explained, "sometimes they [ministers] have dark and difficult cases to manage, and in this way of associating together, they may counsel and encourage and comfort one another. . . . "[54]

Ministerial associations provided isolated clergymen with opportunities for social communion, served as schools of personal authority, helped ministers clarify their obligations to the sick, and provided advice on the more difficult cases of church discipline and controversy. Their functions were less political than social; they were concerned less with exercising power and dominion over the laity than with providing counsel and encouragement to the clergy. "As all Christians are called upon to bear one another's burdens, so should ministers in peculiar manner sympathize with one another, and comfort and encourage one another . . . in all ye ways that they possibly can."[55]

But this is not all. Ministerial associations served yet another function, perhaps their most important. For it was in the ministerial associations that the difficult theological and ecclesiastical problems thrown up by the Great Awakening were confronted and a consensus fashioned. If the Great Awakening did not divide the New England ministry into opposing armies, as Alan Heimert thought; if most clergymen aligned themselves neither with the Old Lights nor with the New Lights, but with the more moderate, middle-of-the-road Regular Lights, as Samuel Mather reported; then a large part of the reason must lie with the ministerial associations. They had grown rapidly during the first three decades of the eighteenth century; by 1740 they covered all of Connecticut and most of Massachusetts. Everywhere they were powerless; everywhere the laity reigned supreme. Yet it was, ironically, their very impotences that allowed them to play a powerfully integrative role during the upheaval of the early 1740s. Lacking real power, they did not become the objects of struggles for power and so were able to avoid strife and contention, polarization and division. Here was the great importance of the ministerial associations.

If this obvious fact has been lost upon recent historians, it is because they have been preoccupied with the search for a domineering elite. But it was not lost upon the members of the Sherburne Association: "Meeting together and conferring with one another" was above all, a "way and means to preserve and maintain peace and unity amongst ye pastors of ye churches."[56] In the following pages we will examine how this was done.

At each meeting the associations typically set questions to be studied and discussed at the following meeting. Some of these were trivial. On 13 October 1747, for example, the Hampshire Association debated the not very pressing question of whether saints could expect to find in Heaven a degree of glory exceeding that of the angels.[57] Similarly, on 20 March 1710/11, the Sherburne Association devoted the entire day to debating the virtues of private prayer.[58]

But these were exceptions. Members took turns proposing questions to be discussed at each meeting, and these questions most often reflected their attempts to apply traditional theological and ecclesiological principles to the pressing problems of the day. In this way the associations served as a mechanism for relating inherited doctrine to practical problems.

The associations also provided a forum to achieve a consensus on that application. Since the associations were not political bodies—since they neither formulated nor executed policy—their sole objective in discussing theological and ecclesiological "first principles" was to resolve differences of opinion and achieve consensus. The associations grew out of that mood of exhaustion—"a mood that had become wearied with great contentions, shameful strifes, grievous divisions"—that settled over the New England clergy in the first decades of the eighteenth century.[59] The system of regularly examining theological and ecclesiological principles and discussing their current applications was initially established, as the Sherburne ministers explained in 1704, "to allay and compose ye differences and divisions that are at anytime amongst ye ministers of ye Gospel."[60]

Given this desire for consensus and union, the ministerial associations, like the town meetings, continued their discussion of every question until a consensus had been achieved. If they remained divided at the end of their meeting, the question was then carried over to the next meeting. Thus the Hampshire ministers, at their meeting on 12 October 1736, found themselves unable to agree on the validity of Roman Catholic baptism and so carried their discussion over to the next meeting. The thorny and difficult problem of admission to communion remained unresolved at the end of the meeting on 28 October 1746 and so was taken up when they next convened.[61] On 5 September 1692 the Boston/Cambridge Association found itself unable to agree on a difficult question and so it was "left to further discourse."[62] Though infrequent, the practice of carrying unresolved questions over to the next meeting suggests the associations' commitment to achieving consensus.

The theological principles discussed usually involved problems that had plagued Calvinism since the early seventeenth century. The Sherburn Association, for example, wrestled with the inherent contradiction between the doctrine of Original Sin and that of Divine Righteousness on 20 October 1713, and six months later with the no less vexing contradiction of urging helpless sinners to be "up and doing," to be involved in a drama of salvation they were unable to influence.[63] The Hampshire Association also discussed the eternal problem of reconciling Original Sin with the justice of God, grappled with the difference between Justification and Sanctification, debated whether grace may lie dormant in an apparently unregerate soul (18 October 1743), argued about whether persons could be converted "without the terms of the law," and a host of similar questions.[64]

By discussing the most basic and fundamental theological principles in this way, New England clergymen were able to maintain a broad consensus of opinion that lasted through and beyond the Great Awakening. "If I have a true idea of things," declared Samuel Niles in 1745,

> our present controversy is not about the fundamental points of religion. All agree in the doctrine of original sin, the necessity of conversion or the New Birth, of justification by faith in the merits of Christ, the imputation of Christ's righteousness received by faith, and good works or an holy obedience as a fruit and evidence of the true faith. All my brethren in the ministry, that I am acquainted with, assent to these doctrines, and preach them to their hearts . . . Moreover, if at any time it has been prov'd against any minister, that his doctrine or life is not according to the gospel, he has by our constitution been removed from his ministry.[65]

Associations devoted a good deal of time to fashioning this theological consensus; they devoted even more time to discussing New England's ecclesiastical principles. And like the discussions devoted to theology, these examinations revolved around questions of fundamental import: the relations of ministers to their congregations; the perennial problem of admission to baptism and communion; and the autonomy of particular churches.

It is important to emphasize that these were not discussions of particular cases, but of broad principles. The questions were always set at an abstract level; at the same time, the attempt was obviously to arrive at principles that could actually be applied in a variety of situations. On 4 April 1692, for example, the Boston/Cambridge Association approached the problem of ruling elders in this way: "What are the gifts absolutely necessary to ruling elders, and what the works to be attended by such elders in the churches of our Lord, and how are they to be chosen and ordained there unto?"[66]

And as with problems of theology, the attempt to arrive at a consensus can be seen in the fact that particularly difficult problems were brought up again and again, until agreement had been reached. The Bradford Association, for instance, discussed the Cambridge Platform at its meeting on 21 June 1720 but found agreement so elusive that they devoted three more meetings to the question.[67] The fact that, in 1751, not one Hampshire Association minister followed Jonathan Edwards in restricting communion to visible saints may have been partially due to the fact that the Association had devoted two successive meetings in the late 1740s to resolving their differences of opinion on that very question.[68] It is doubtful that Edwards would have been swayed by these discussions. But he was absent, and his absence must have made it easier for the remaining clergymen to arrive at the consensus they later displayed. That consensus was surely one of the reasons that Edwards, when an ecclesiastical council was chosen to examine the dispute, sent all the way to Boston for clerical allies.[69] In the end the Boston ministers failed to show up, the council was composed almost entirely of Hampshire County ministers, and they unanimously rejected Edwards' position.[70] On both theological and ecclesiastical problems, the associations worked to achieve a consensus among their members. Their meetings and particularly their discussions of abstract principles, as the Sherburne ministers testified, "tend very much to allay their hearts and to moderate and compose and calm and quiet their spirits, and so . . . tend to ye allaying and composing of their differences and contentions."[71]

None of the extant records of the ministerial associations reveal the actual give and take of these debates. We have their statements that associations were formed to discuss basic principles, moderate differences of opinion and achieve consensus; we can see that they established and maintained procedures designed to do that; and we can see that they were to a large degree successful – by the consensus on theological and ecclesiastical principles described in the earlier chapters, and because their associations, like the town meetings, almost always concluded their discussions with phrases like, "we all concurred," or "we agreed," or "all did agree," or "it was agreed."   But the actual fashioning of that agreement lies beyond our view.

Nevertheless, we can catch an occasional glimpse of the process. We should note, first, that because of their lack of real power, clergymen were extremely sensitive to the dangers of factionalism. They often used the metaphor of an "earthen vessel" to describe their profession – a metaphor that reveals their fear that the ministry might be broken to pieces by contention. For ministers "to strike one against another," as John White of Gloucester pointed out in 1725, "'tis not without the utmost peril of the breaking and sinking of both."[72]   This fear of factionalism gripped the minds of New England clergymen like a vice. The Sherburne Association devoted its session of 21 March 1704 to the question, "What are the woful effects of division among the ministers of the Gospel,"[73] and their next meeting to examining ways these divisions could be overcome.[74]   Even laymen pointed out how vulnerable the clergy were on this score. In *A Letter to the Clergy*,[75] an anonymous layman warned that "nothing sinks the Reputation of the ministry more than for them to revile and reproach each other. No wonder, in that case, if we of the laity have a low opinion of you, when you seem to have so very low an opinion of yourselves."

This obsessive fear of factionalism within their profession was not confined to Liberal clergymen; it haunted even the New Lights. John White of Gloucester, mentioned above, is a good example, as is Eleazar Wheelock of Lebanon, Connecticut. Contentions between clergymen renders the ministry "a house divided against itself which cannot stand," Wheelock warned. "Intestine jarrs all-ways weaken the whole body, and in this case it does it in too many respects to relate."[76] Even a firebrand like Andrew Croswell worried "lest those who are *Antiministerial . . .* should get any Advantage by my Writings, and strengthen themselves in a Way that is not good."[77]   For these reasons, as the Sherburn ministers pointed out, "the ministers of Christ should, of all men, be extraordinarily careful to maintain peace and unity amongst themselves."[78]

Ministers who remained insensitive or indifferent to the need for

unity, who "care not what others think of them," seemed, to Zabdiel
Adams and probably to most other ministers, to be possessed by "a base
and sordid mind, of a low and grovelling soul, but just raised above the
level of the brutal creation."[79] Ministers "should consider what will be
ye sad and woful effects of their divisions" and "what obligations they
are [therefore] under to live in love and peace."[80]

It was against this fear of factionalism and the consequent desire for
unity that ministerial associations went about their business. The sermons
ad clerum preached by each clergyman in turn were designed not to
delineate and sharpen differences but to "ally and compose divisions."
The discourse that John Sergeant of Stockbridge preached to the
Hampshire Association on 13 April 1743, at the very zenith of the Great
Awakening, was in this respect typical, as was its reception.   "The
Association of ministers in this county set this week in Springfield," one
of Wheelock's correspondents informed him, "and the Rev. Mr. Sergeant
of Stockbrige preached a public lecture this day . . . a very gentle,
healing sermon, I believe to the universal satisfaction both of ministers
and people."[81]

This is not to say that association meetings were always harmonious
affairs; they were not. Especially during the early years of the
Awakening, they often erupted into acrimonious debate. But there is no
evidence that any of them were polarized or broken into pieces by these
disputes, and that is the more important point.   In every case the
differences were composed and the associations preserved. Consider the
disagreement within the Marlborough Association precipitated by
Whitefield's return to New England in 1745. On 22 January of that year
the Association met at Marlborough and discussed whether to draw up a
memorial protesting Whitefield's approaching visit. Ebenezer Parkman
of Westborough argued against the idea. No consensus having been
achieved, the question was carried over to the next meeting, on 11 June.
This time "a sharp and vehement" argument occurred, and Parkman
threatened to resign. Only "after long contest" did he withdraw his resig-
nation. No further mention was made of the memorial against Whitefield.[82]

Another entry in Parkman's *Diary* reveals a similar effort, similarly
successful, to moderate and soften conviction in the interests of ministerial harmony and unity. At the Marlborough Association's meeting of 4
October 1768, the Rev. Joseph Buckminster of Rutland, in Parkman's
words,

> seemed to be too much of an Advocate—I gave him some hint in the
> assembly—at eve he somewhat resented it—but Mr. Stiles gave him to understand
> that it was the mind of others, which I had delivered—he was afterwards silent

about it and reformed.   He was very instrumental afterwards in accomplishing a coalition.[83]

Or, finally, consider the controversy that surrounded John Martyn's settlement at Northborough in 1745. Martyn was a strict Calvinist, while the Marlborough Association displayed a distinctly liberal coloration. Early in 1745 the Northfield Church asked the Association for its advice on settling Martyn.   He accordingly appeared before that body and delivered "a large Confession of Faith" on 9 March, to which the Rev. John Gardner of Stow objected. The ensuing debate occupied the entire day and continued into the next. Finally "Mr. Gardner and he were advised to retire together. They did so and came in reconciled." In the afternoon "We [had] further debate, and were more successful and pacified." At the end of the day Martyn "was approbated by a Certificate signed by every member."[84]

These few instances are obviously not conclusive. But when combined with the larger pattern of association activities described above, they suggest that ministerial associations existed not to augment the power of the ministers but to overcome their individual isolation, maintain a consensus of opinion on inherited doctrine, and preserve clerical unity. If the New England clergy was not divided into warring camps, as Alan Heimert and others have contended; if the great bulk of ministers were "Regular Lights," as Samuel Mather, Ezra Stiles and others believed; then the mechanism by which that broad "middle way" was preserved was the ministerial associations. As Joseph Baxter explained, "As [ministers'] strangenesse to one another tends to alienate their minds and affections from one another, so their meeting together and conferring with one another, and kindly treating one another tends to maintain and promote love and peace and unity among them."[85] Thus we can understand Ezra Stiles when, in 1760, he urged his colleagues to "rejoice that we are so well agreed in purity of doctrine and worship . . . we are and continue, united in faith and fellowship."[86]

Old Calvinism, Millennialism and Revolution: The Vision of Ezra Stiles

In the last ten years, historians of American thought have become increasingly aware of the role of millennialism in the formation of a revolutionary mentality in the 1770s. The struggle against British tyranny was perceived by many eighteenth-century Americans as a crucial phase in the cosmic battle between God and Antichrist for the soul of mankind. Victory over British arms would not only save America from vice and corruption, but would begin a new chapter in God's work of redeeming the world. Americans, it seemed, were being "raised up to God, and divinely formed by a peculiar influence of the sovereign of the Universe" for the "accomplishment of the *Magnalia Dei* . . . in these of the earth." The American Revolution, as Alan Heimert suggests in his *Religion and the American Mind*, "was not so much the result of reasoned thought as an emotional outburst, similar to a religious revival."[1]

The presence of millennial modes of thought in the revolutionary mentality now seems well established. But identifying the source of that millenialism has proven more difficult. Heimert argued that the millennialism of the revolutionary era grew directly out of the religious expectations aroused by the New Lights during the Great Awakening, that the communitarian nature of their millennial vision led them, in the popular mobilization of the late 1760s and 1770s, to confuse "civic virtue with piety, and finally, political enthusiasm with the joy of conversion." Other historians have found the source of revolutionary era millennialism in different groups and places. Nathan Hatch has found that millennial expectations were expressed by rationalists as well as pietists. William McLoughlin has argued that the Baptists, too, were an important source of millennial enthusiasm.[2]

It is not only the source of revolutionary millennialism that is in doubt; the way in which the spiritual millennialism of the Awakening was transformed into the "civil" or "civic" millennialism of the revolutionary era is also a matter of dispute. How was a style of thought born of spiritual expectation able to mobilize large numbers of Americans for a struggle for "natural rights"? How did the goal of national independence eclipse the hope of advancing God's kingdom on earth? Or, more accurately, how did they become confused with one another, how did they come to mean one and the same thing? How were the eschatological expectations of the 1740s secularized and politicized in the thirty years between the Great Awakening and the American Revolution?

Heimert argued, as we have seen, that it was the Revolutionary crisis itself, and the mobilization of popular sentiment that accompanied it, that transformed the hope of redemption into political terms. It was "through the confounding of piety with political enthusiasm" that the millennial vision of the New Lights "came to center on the crisis in public affairs, and, indeed, to be defined by it and from it to derive vitality." Hatch, on the other hand, contends that the crucial transformation had been accomplished ten to fifteen years earlier, in the Great War for Empire. Both New Lights and Old Lights equated the struggle between Protestant England and Catholic France with the cosmic battle between God and Anti-Christ, and the effect of that identification was to politicize the millennial impulse. The defeat of the French Anti-Christ was seen to be an essential step in God's work of redemption. McLoughlin contends that the politicization of Baptist millennialism had less to do with the war against France than with the Baptists' struggle against the Standing Order of the New England churches.[3]

In this chapter I suggest that another, and I think a more obvious, source of revolutionary era millennialism lay in the ecclesiastical thought of the Old Calvinists. The Great Awakening generated among them, as it did among the New Lights, a fervent belief that America was destined to become God's new Zion, that the new world had been specially reserved for "the most glorious designs of Providence." But whereas the New Lights thought "this great work" would be accomplished by way of a massive revival of piety—what Jonathan Edwards called "a glorious pouring out of the Spirit"—the Old Calvinists saw it as a product of gradual ecclesiastical purification superimposed upon the increasing demographic superiority of the Congregational and Presbyterian establishments in the northern and middle colonies. Moreover, the Old Calvinists defined the millennium not as an indwelling of the spirit, as the New Lights were wont to do, but as a recovery of "the ecclesiastical polity instituted and delivered by the holy Apostles." This formulation grew directly out of the experiences of the 1740s and 1750s. By channeling the energies released by the Great Awakening into existing ecclesiastical forms, and by using the ministerial associations as forums for discussing the "fit" between ecclesiastical form and ecclesiastical principle, the clergy gave those forms a new legitimacy and a new stability. Just as individual congregations often renewed their church covenants, so it seemed that the religious culture as a whole had renewed its commitment to New England's "Middle Way." The Great Awakening thus gave New England clergymen a renewed sense of their place and role in history. Providence, it seemed in 1760, had "reserved the honor of a most purified reformation for [the] churches in New England."[4] During the 1760s this celebration was developed into a special kind of millennialism — what I here call "institutional millennialism" — that combined the enthusiasm of a chiliastic vision with a reverence for the standing order. This institutional millennialism provided the link connecting the Great Awakening with the Revolution. In the pages that follow I compare and contrast the institutional millennialism of the Old Calvinists with the more spiritual millenialism of the New Lights, and then show how this institutional millennialism contributed to the formation of a revolutionary disposition in the 1770s.

I

Early in October of 1757, the trustees of the College of New Jersey offered the presidency of that institution to Jonathan Edwards, who was then serving as a missionary to the Indians at Stockbridge, Massachusetts. Edwards was reluctant to accept the presidency. Though his work with the Indians had been crowned with "no remarkable visible success," he had found a peaceful situation in which to pursue his theological studies. Free from the distractions of parish duties and inter-church affairs, Edwards was able to devote himself to theology "more closely and to better purpose than ever." During his stay at Stockbridge he wrote more than during any comparable period of his life, and both of his masterpieces, *Treatise on the Will* and *On Original Sin*, were completed there.[5]

Moreover, he had recently begun a work which, as he told the trustees, had "long engaged and swallowed up my mind . . . a great work which I call *A History of the Work of Redemption*." This was to be a work of theology "in an entire new method, being thrown into the form of a history." In it, Edwards undertook not only to record the past events of God's work in the world, but also to elucidate the events which were to precede the final "consummation of all things." It was, as the historian C. C. Goen has suggested, "a radical innovation which had decisive consequences for the future."[6]

It was Edwards' conviction, as displayed in the *History*, that the end of the world would be preceded by a gradual redemption of mankind, a period of great holiness, happiness and prosperity *on earth*. There was nothing new in this belief. The early Christian sects had also believed that history would culminate in a period of temporal felicity. But that belief had been submerged in the early middle ages. When the travail and sufferings of the early church had made it obvious that the golden age was not immediately at hand, Christian theologians had reformulated the idea. The millennium was taken out of time, out of human history, to stand as the City of God, in shining contrast to the earthly City of Man.[7]

In the early years of the seventeenth century the English theologian Joseph Mede revived the earlier idea of an earthly millenium *in* history and preceding the end of the world. This revival accorded with and gave religious sanction to the historical optimism of the seventeenth century. The idea was further refurbished and refined by Henry More, Thomas Burnet, Daniel Whitby, Charles Daubuz, Moses Lowman and other seventeenth-century English biblical commentators until, by the end of the century, its popularity had become "overwhelming."[8] In his study of New England eschatology, Perry Miller suggested that Edwards drew his ideas about the millennium from his reading of Isaac Newton and other physicists. But it now seems that he drew directly upon the English millennial scholars mentioned above. In any case, his achievement was new and unexpected in the American context.[9]

Edwards envisioned God's redemption of the world as a gradual process that began with Christ's resurrection and proceeded "in various steps from that time to the end of the world." There were four decisive events in this scenario: Christ's appearance on earth and his resurrection from the dead; the conversion of Constantine; the Protestant Reformation and the eventual destruction of the Popish Antichrist that it foreordained; and God's final judgment. Each of these events Edwards regarded as "so many steps and degrees of the accomplishment of one great event," i.e., "in each one of them the event is accomplished in a further degree than in the foregoing." The significance of his own time was thus made clear: having inherited the reforms of the Reformation, the eighteenth century looked forward to the fall of Antichrist which would mark the end of the third stage and usher in the millennium preceding the final judgment. Moreover, this perspective gave a cosmic dynamism to the years of his own lifetime. Edwards actually felt the very "heaven and earth shaking, that the new heavens and new earth, which cannot be shaken, may be established and remain." The times, it seemed, were pregnant with divine intentions.[10]

Like the Great Awakening that had precipitated these speculations, the millennium itself would be ushered in by a great revival of piety. "The great work," Edwards announced, "shall be accomplished, not by the authority of princes, nor by the wisdom of learned men, but by God's Holy Spirit." Edwards' descriptions make it evident that he saw the approach of the golden age as a version of the Great Awakening played out on a universal scale. "The pouring out of the Spirit of God" would

> soon bring great multitudes to forsake the vice and wickedness which now so generally prevails, and shall cause that vital religion which is now so despised and laughed at in the world, to revive . . . the work of conversion shall go on in a wonderful manner, and spread more and more. Many shall flow together to the goodness of the Lord, and shall come as it were in flocks, one flock and multitude after another continually flowing in . . . and it shall spread more and more with wonderful swiftness, and vast numbers shall suddenly be brought in as it were at once.[11]

The millennium, Edwards proclaimed, "will be a time of great light and knowledge." And of great holiness: "vital religion shall everywhere prevail," as well as "great peace and love." The nations of the earth will throw down their arms and "be knit together in sweet harmony." Rulers and ruled will embrace and all men "will be abundant in expressing their love one to another." "Malice, and envy, and wrath, and revenge [shall] be suppressed everywhere," mankind will enjoy "the greatest temporal prosperity," and "all the world [shall] be united in one amiable society."[12]

Not only did the millennium seem imminent; it also seemed destined to commence in America. What brought Edwards to this conviction was not only the intensity of the Great Awakening in this country but common sense as well. Since Christ had been born in the Old World, and since "Providence observes a kind of equal distribution of things," it seemed "not unlikely" that "the glorious application of redemption is to begin in this." Besides, the Old World had crucified Christ and thereby forfeited its role in the work of redemption. And had not the Old World been the source of men's material wealth for ages? Just so, the New would be the scene of spiritual treasures beyond description. Had not the Old World been the arena of man's corruption? So the New would be the scene of his redemption. And does it not stand to reason that God should begin this work "in a wilderness, where nothing grows and nothing is to be seen but dry and barren rocks?" Even the apparent coincidents of history seemed to confirm the judgment: had America not been discovered "about the time of the reformation, or but little before?"

So that as soon as this new world is (as it were) created, and stands forth in view, God presently goes about doing some great thing to make way for the introduction of the church's latter day glory, that is to have its first seat in, and is to take its rise from that new world.[13]

Edwards' millennialism was inspired by the revivals of the Great Awakening. The millennium would, he believed, be inaugurated by an outpouring of God's spirit and it would consist of a renewal of "the hearts and minds of mankind." It would come "neither by a reconstruction of the temple nor through its destruction, but as a renewal of the nature of those who dwelt within."

But when "the fires of the revival flickered and went out," Edwards abandoned his hopes for America and turned his attention to Europe, where the revival of piety had suffered no such decline. Other New Lights either abandoned millennialism entirely or took the millennial age out of history completely. The New Light millennial vision, as Hatch remarks,

could never have provided the intellectual foundation for the historical optimism prevalent among ministers of the Revolutionary era. Based on the sources of awakened piety, it could not sustain the interest of a generation whose infatuation with revivalism faded as quickly as it had flowered.[14]

Old Calvinist millennialism, on the other hand, was less spiritual and therefore more capable of inspiring the civil millennialism of the 1770s. Ezra Stiles, like Edwards, believed that the end of the world would be preceded by a period of unparalleled holiness and human happiness, that history was progressive in that it revealed the gradual redemption of mankind and that it would culminate in an earthly millennium. Upon the completion of "three coetaneous events" ("the annihilation of the Pontificate; the reassembling of the Jews; and the fulness of the Gentiles") God "will burst forth" to convert the world and redeem mankind. The "time will come," Stiles proclaimed, when "the most glorious designs of Providence" will be accomplished, "filling the earth with the knowledge of the glory of the Lord." Heaven had put a stop to the propagation of Christianity under the Popes. But once the Pontificate had been finally destroyed and Christianity "recovered to the primitive purity and simplicity" of the early church, "the human race shall be ready to drop their idolatry, and all false religion [and] Christianity shall triumph over superstition as well as Deism, Gentilism and Mahometism." Missionaries will then "be blessed to succeed" in their work, the newly converted gospelized heathen will "light up their candle," and "instead of the Bable [of] confusion" all mankind "will harmoniously concur in speaking one language, one holy faith, one apostolick religion. . . . " Though Stiles did not believe the millennium to be imminent, as did Edwards, neither did he consign it to a vague and indefinite future time. In 1762 he thought the golden age would appear in 350 years and in 1769 he revised that estimate to 600 years. In 1783 he worked over his figures once again and announced that the millennium would commence in "seven or eight hundred years. . . . "[15]

And like Edwards in his early millennialism, Stiles confidently expected that the golden age would commence in America. "We have reason to think," he explained, "that the United States may be of no small influence and consideration in effecting this great event . . . I doubt not this is the honour reserved for us: I had almost said in the spirit of prophecy, the zeal of the Lord of Hosts will accomplish this." Had God not sent the Jews into the wilderness to prepare a place for the Lord? In a similar way "it may have been of the Lord" that the church was exiled into the wilderness of America to cleanse itself of Popish corruption and prepare for "the unmolested accomplishment of the Magnalia Dei," which had been "designed from eternal ages to be displayed in these ends of the earth."

> In this country, out of sight of mitres and the purple, and removed from systems of corruption confirmed for ages . . . revelation, both as to the true evangelical doctrines, and church polity, may be settled . . . of this it gives me joy to believe there is the greatest prospect.[16]

But Stiles' millennialism was of a fundamentally different sort than that articulated by Edwards and the New Lights. In Stiles' version, God will pour down his blessings only after the church had cleansed itself and been restored to its "Apostolick purity." The millennium was to be advanced not by propagating piety and revivalism, but by rebuilding the holy temple. On this Stiles was quite explicit. All attempts to redeem mankind "shall prove fruitless until the present Christiandom itself shall be recovered to the primitive purity and simplicity." Only when "the mutilated, artificial forms of the pontificate or patriarchal constitutions" had been totally expunged and the church once again set upon the apostolic model would God commence the millennial age. Herein lay the distinctiveness of Old Calvinist millennialism and the reason it was able to extend itself beyond the temporary spiritualism of the Great Awakening. For, by stressing ecclesiastical form and structure, Stiles made his millennialism a product of human endeavour in a way that Edwards would never have done. In the scriptures, men possessed an exact blueprint for the kind of churches they were intended to create.

The inauguration of the golden age waited not upon a renewal of the spirit, not upon defeat of French armies, but solely upon the reformation of ecclesiastical form.[17]

Moreover, this emphasis provided a firmer foundation for the belief that America would be the staging area for the millennial age. For, if that great event was to be inaugurated where the church had been most thoroughly reformed, Stiles allowed himself no doubts that it would begin in America. Europe had begun the work of reformation; America would see its final culmination. "When the church was entirely corrupted in the papacy He raised up and spirited the Reformation. But to me," Stiles explained in 1760, "it appears that He has reserved the honour of a most purified reformation for our churches in New England."[18]

This is not to say that Stiles thought the New England churches completely renovated and restored to their original purity and simplicity. He readily admitted that "we need indeed some further purification and amendments." But he thought these "will doubtless take place in the process of time," that "the next capital change will be to a still greater purity, both in doctrine and worship."[19]

Three interrelated factors allowed him this confidence. One was the present state of the established churches. "I am persuaded," Stiles wrote in 1760, "that there is no body of churches in the Protestant world more nearly recovered to the simplicity and purity of the Apostolick age" than those in New England. The second factor had to do with civil authority. The "imperfections" still plaguing the New England churches would be "much more easily amended than in any other Protestant church" because "amendments [will] not be encountered with the like opposition of authorities and unwieldy temporalities." Separatists, Baptists, Quakers and others would not have agreed, of course. But according to Stiles, they had abandoned the quest for scriptural authenticity by denying the validity of presbyterian ordination, which Stiles thought lay at the very center of the "Apostolick model." It was the Congregational and Presbyterian establishment that Stiles had in mind when he spoke of the purity of the New England churches; it was they who would carry the burden of reformation.[20]

And it was these churches that seemed, to Stiles, to be growing most quickly, which furnished the third reason for optimism on his part. Here Stiles brought his considerable skill in demography to bear. Projecting 1760 growth figures to the end of the eighteenth century, he found that the Congregational and Presbyterian churches would together include seven million communicants, while the Baptists numbered a bare 352,000 and all other denominations registered even smaller numbers.

"There is no body of Christians on earth," Stiles exclaimed in 1760, who are "in such a rapid increase and in so flourishing a state, as the Congregationalists of New England." The purity of their ecclesiastical forms, the absence of impediments to further reform, and the future expansion of the Congregational churches all contributed to give Stiles a bouyant view of the future. The New England churches seemed to be "advancing forward, by an augmented natural increase and spiritual edifications, into a singular superiority. . . . "

> The initial revival of this primeval institution is indeed already so well established here, . . . that there can be but little doubt, but that in the ordinary course of events, our increasing and growing interest, without any interference with the other sects, will at length ascent to such magnitude, and become so great and respectable a part of Christendom, as to command the attention, contemplation, and fraternal love of our brethren and fellow Christians, of the church universal, and even of the world itself.

Stiles considered any further projections unnecessary, since this "ordinary course of events" will have "advanced us into the millennial times."[21]

Stiles' answer to the theological controversies of the 1750s had been, as we have seen, to translate them into ecclesiastical arguments and then propose his ideal of congregational autonomy as a resolution. But this was more than a strategem; the autonomy of individual congregations seemed to him the very essence of what he called "the Apostolick model." "The churches were really congregational from the beginning," he declared in the *Discourse on Christian Union* in 1760. All antiquity confessed the part which the people had in the election of their pastors and in admitting members to communion. This was also the manner and form prescribed by New England's founding generation. "It was a fundamental principle" among them,

> that every voluntary assembly of Christians had power to form, organize and govern themselves, and in imitation of the apostolic churches, to gather and incorporate themselves by a public covenant, and to elect and ordain all their officers.

Thus, "if there be any true way of worshipping the Diety," it seemed that "it may be in our way." All other forms of church organization were "of modern date and defensible only upon these novel interpretations which are subversive of [this] first grand, fundamental principle."[22]

This applied with special force to extra-congregational structures of authority. The crowning achievement of the Protestant Reformation had been, for Stiles, its reassertion of congregational autonomy, its belief in the integrity of the individual Christian community against the claims of Rome. It was a belief that always stood in the forefront of his thinking on ecclesiastical matters. "If we once depart from the plenary power of churches over their oficers," he warned in 1771, "we may adopt a principle which will justify the pontificate." When he received, early in February of 1771, a proposal to erect a consociation of churches in the vicinity of Salem, Massachusetts, he replied that "men of all ages have endeavoured to aggrandize themselves on the ruins of the church's liberties." The proposal seemed to be based on "a principle upon which one might ascend to the all comprehensive and all absorbing policy of the Pontificant." To his diary he confided that he was "apprehensive" of "this Salem Witchcraft."[23]

Thus, ironically, the very purity of the New England churches — their autonomy both from one another and from any superintending authority — left them isolated and vulnerable to subversion by schemes like the Salem proposal. Stiles believed that once the dynamic of projected population growth caught hold, their vulnerability would be remedied by the strength of numbers. But until that time he saw the churches as a tender young vine in a hostile wilderness. These churches are "vigilantly to be guarded" Stiles warned in 1760. "It is incumbent upon us to watch and guard their infancy with a paternal, God-like fidelity." It was "truly important that this vine which God hath planted with a mighty hand in this American wilderness should be cultivated into confirmed maturity," for upon its growth rested the hope of inaugurating the millennium in America.[24]

For this reason, Stiles watched the development of the Church of England in America with increasing alarm. It was not the number of Anglican converts that worried him as much as their class composition. As early as 1759 he warned of the Anglicans' tendency to engage "persons of influence and opulence." He became preoccupied with the relative wealth of Anglican communicants, comparing parish lists with tax rolls in various cities and noting the results in his diary. By establishing a base among the colonial elite, the Anglicans, he reasoned, hoped to capture political control of the colonies, establish "a juncture of the civil and episcopal powers," launch "a formal attempt on the chastity and order of our churches," "bring the Church of England into Supremacy in New England," and thereby bring the process of reformation and purification to an end, and with it all, hope of seeing the millennium inaugurated in America.[25]

In the summer of 1771 a dispute erupted in an Anglican church that vividly illustrated, for Stiles, the potential danger of an Anglican establishment. The Reverend Mather Byles, Jr.'s Anglican congregation in Boston had guaranteed him an annual salary of £100. After this settlement had been sealed, the Anglican Society for the Propagation of the Gospel offered Byles another £40 per annum, which he accepted. When the congregation learned of this offer they communicated to Byles' their intention to reduce his salary accordingly. "Upon which," Stiles recorded in his diary, Byles

> shut up the church doors last Spring for two sabbaths and a fast; and at the same time engaged the rest of the Episcopalian Clergy in town not to preach for the Congregation.

But the congregation was adamant. After remonstrating with the priest, they set about arrangements to drop their Anglican affiliation and hire a Congregational minister.

> This brought Byles to himself. He immdiately went cap in hand to the heads of the congregation and told them, he humbly tendered them his services, in the name of the Lord Jesus. Upon which they received him again.

The Anglicans had been defeated in this episode, but it made a lasting impression on Stiles. "It shows," he wrote in his diary, "that if they were well and firmly invested with power they would subjugate the churches."[26]

For Ezra Stiles, the struggle for independence was not an attempt to reassert the rights of Englishmen, nor an effort to salvage the corrupted English constitution, but another step in God's ancient plan to redeem mankind and inaugurate a holy millennium on earth. The prism through which he saw the conflict, the apocalyptic imagery he used to describe it, betrayed the archaic understandings of an utterly traditional mind. America was "God's new Israel"; Anglican priests and British officials were agents of the Antichrist, desperate to arrest the reformation of Christianity that had come so close to completion in his new biblical wilderness. In the history of the universe they "will be considered as the Pharaohs, the Zamzummins, the Nebuchanezzars, the Plagues of a holy people." Americans, so nearly recovered to apostolic purity and simplicity in their churches, were now being pursued by Pharoah and his hosts. "There remains," he knew, "only for us to stand still and see the salvation of the God of our fathers."[27]

Stiles believed America to be "God's new Israel" not because a revival of New Light piety had spread across the land, nor because such a vision had been awakened during the Great War for Empire, but because, as he never tired of explaining, "there is no body of churches in the Protestant world more nearly recovered to the simplicity and purity of the apostolic age." The contribution of the Old Calvinists to the revolutionary mentality of the 1770s was to stress, once again, that the mission of America, the means by which it was to redeem mankind and inaugurate the millennial age, was not to gather the saints out of the world, but to build "a city on a hill."[28]

Notes

Introduction

1. C.C. Goen, ed., *The Works of Jonathan Edwards*, vol. 4 (New Haven, 1972), p. 344.

2. Ibid., p. 350.

3. Ibid.

4. Edwards to the Rev. James Robe, 12 May 1743, in Ibid., p. 536.

5. Edwin Gaustad, *The Great Awakening in New England* (Chicago, 1968), p. 82; Alan Heimert, *Religion and the American Mind* (Cambridge, 1966) pp. 3, 8; Paul R. Lucas, *Valley of Discord: Church and Society along the Connecticut River, 1636-1725* (Hanover, 1976), p. 202; James Schmotter, "Provincial Professionalism: The New England Ministry, 1692-1745" (Unpublished Ph.D. dissertation, Northwestern University, 1973), pp. 283, 310; Cedric B. Cowing, *The Great Awakening and the American Revolution: Colonial Thought in the Eighteenth-Century* (Chicago, 1972, 1971), pp. 65, 73-74; Richard L. Bushman, ed., *The Great Awakening: Documents on the Revival of Religion, 1740-1745* (New York, 1970), p. 133.

6. Gaustad, *The Great Awakening*, p. 81; Goen, ed., *Works*, vol. 4, pp. 116, 148.

7. Goen, ed., *Works*, vol. 4, pp. 223, 503.

8. Gaustad, *The Great Awakening*, pp. 81.

9. Ibid., p. 82.

10. Cowing, *The Great Awakening*, p. 66; Harry Stout, "The Great Awakening in New England Reconsidered: The New England Clergy," *Journal of Social History*: 8 (Fall, 1974), 21-47. Stout divides the entire New England clergy into New Light and Old Light camps. See pp. 22-23 and 43-44.

11. Heimert, *Religion and the American Mind*, pp. 3-9; Gaustad, *The Great Awakening*, pp. 80-101; Richard Niebuhr, *The Kingdom of God in America* (Chicago, 1937),

p. 126.   The phrase in quotation marks is from Bernard Bailyn's *The Ordeal of Thomas Hutchinson* (London, 1975), p. ix.

12.   Samuel Mather, *The State of Religion in New England* . . . (Glasgow, 1742), passim, but especially pp. 14 and 42.   See also Ezra Stiles, *Extracts from Itineraries, with Selections from His Correspondence*, ed. F.B. Dexter (Boston, 1916), p. 414.

13.   Clifford Shipton, *Sibley's Harvard Graduates*, vol. 4 (Boston, 1942), pp. 521-22; Ebenezer Parkman, *The Diary of Ebenezer Parkman*, ed. Francis G. Walett (Worcester, 1974), entries for 22 January and 11 June 1745, pp. 110 and 119.

14.   Ebenezer Parkman to Andrew Eliot, 14 July 1743, Commonplace Book, in Francis Parkman Papers, Massachusetts Historical Society.

15.   *The Testimony of the Pastors of the Churches in the Province of the Massachusetts-Bay . . . May 25, 1743 . . .* (Boston, 1743).

16.   *The Testimony and Advice of an Assembly of Pastors . . . July 7, 1743 . . .* (Boston, 1743).

17.   Ebenezer Parkman to William Cooper, 14 July 1743, Commonplace Book, Massachusetts Historical Society.

18.   Parkman to Andrew Eliot, 14 July 1743, Commonplace Book, Massachusetts Historical Society.

19.   John Sibley, *Biographical Sketches* . . . vol. 3 (Cambridge, 1885) p. 437; William B. Sprague, *Annals of the American Pulpit* . . . vol. 1 (New York, 1859), pp. 238-41.

20.   John Hancock, *An Expostulatory and Pacifick Letter* . . . (Boston, 1743), pp. 5, 7.

21.   Daniel Walker Howe, "The Decline of Calvinism: An Approach to Its Study," *Comparative Studies in Society and History*: 14 (June, 1972) 306-27.   For comments on Tennent's retraction, see Jonathan Dickinson to Thomas Foxcroft, 12 April 1742, in Foxcroft Papers, Princeton University.   Tennet's retraction was printed in the *Boston News Letter*, 15-22 July 1742.   On Davenport's "oddities," see Stephen Williams to Eleazur Wheelock, March 16, 1740/41. Wheelock Papers, Dartmouth College Achives, Dartmouth College, *Boston Evening Post*, 5 July 1742; Solomon Williams to Wheelock, 17 July 1741, Wheelock Papers, *Boston Weekly News Letter*, July 19, 1742; Dickinson to Foxcroft, 27 July 1742 and February, 1743; Solomon Williams and Eleazar Wheelock, *Two Letters* . . . (Boston, 1744).   On Ezra Stiles' piety, see Edmund Morgan, *The Gentle Puritan: A Life of Ezra Stiles* (1962), pp. 168-71, 175, and F.B. Dexter, ed., *Literary Diary* (New Haven, 1910), entries for August 4, 7, 8, 1770 and June 25 and 26, 1771.

22.   On the growth of Separatist, Baptist and Anglican churches in New England before the Revolution, see Stiles, *Itineraries*, pp. 92-94 and 352.   On Chauncy's abandonment of orthodoxy, see Shipton, *Sibley's Harvard Graduates*, vol. 6, pp. 456-57.

23. Ezra Stiles, *Discourse on the Christian Union*... (Boston, 1761), pp. 95, 115.

24. Francis Christie, "The Beginnings of Arminianism in New England," *Papers of the American Society of Church History* 2nd series, 3 (1912): 159; Robert G. Pope, "New England Versus the New England Mind: The Myth of Declension," *Journal of Social History:* 3 (1969-1970): 108; Morgan, *The Gentle Puritan*, p. 18; Wright, *The Beginnings of Unitarianism in America* (Boston, 1955), passim; Goodwin, "The Myth of 'Arminian-Calvinism'," *New England Quarterly* 41 (1968): 213-37; Goen, *Works*, pp. 7-9.

25. Mather quoted by Goen, ed., *Works* vol. 4, p. 7; Stiles, *Discourse on The Christian Union*, pp. 51-52; Niles, *Tristitalae Ecclesiarum*... (Boston, 1745), pp. 15-19.

26. David Hall, *The Faithful Shepherd: A History of the New England Ministry in the Seventeenth-Century* (New York, 1972, 1974), p. 288. See also Hall's comment, on page 281, that the "typology of evangelicals versus liberals for the eighteenth century is inadequate."

Chapter 1

1. The standard accounts of the Great Awakening in New England are: Alan Heimert, *Religion and the American Mind: From the Great Awakening to the Revolution* (Harvard University Press, 1966); Edwin Gaustad, *The Great Awakening in New England* (Chicago, 1957); Richard L. Bushman, *From Puritan to Yankee: Character and the Social Order in Connecticut, 1690-1765* (New York, 1967).

2. See Clifford Shipton's sketch of Mather, in his *Sibley's Harvard Graduates*, vol. 7, pp. 216-38. [Samuel Mather], *The State of Religion in New England . . .* (Glasgow, 1742), passim, but especially pp. 14 and 42.

3. Stiles, *Extracts from Itineraries, with Selection from His Correspondence*, F.B. Dexter ed. (Boston, 1916), p. 414; *The Testimony of the Pastors . . . May 25, 1743 . . .* (Boston, 1743). Historians differ on the numerical strength of the moderates. Edwin Gaustad considers them to have been a dwindling minority (*The Great Awakening in New England*, pp. 129-30). Richard Bushman thinks they may have constituted a majority of the Awakening's supporters (*From Puritan to Yankee*, p. 209). However, neither Gaustad nor Bushman – nor anyone else to my knowledge – has ever presented any figures.

4. Willard J. Hurst, *The Growth of American Law: The Lawmakers* (1950); Richard H. Shryock, *Medicine and Society in America, 1660-1860* (1960); David Hall, *The Faithful Shepherd: A History of the New England Ministry in the Seventeenth-Century* (New York, 1972); J. William T. Youngs, *God's Messengers: Religious Leadership in Colonial New England, 1700-1750* (Baltimore, 1976); James W. Schmotter, "Provincial Professionalism: The New England Ministry, 1692-1745" (Unpublished Ph.D. dissertation, Northwestern University, 1973); Alf E. Jacobson, "The Congregational Clergy in Eighteenth-Century New England" (Unpublished Ph.D. dissertation, Harvard University, 1962); Paul R. Luca, *Valley of Discord: Church and Society along the Connecticut River, 1636-1725* (Hanover, 1976). The

final comment in the paragraph is from Harry S. Stout, "The Great Awakening in New England Reconsidered," *Journal of Social History* 8 (1974): 22.

5. Schmotter, "Provincial Professionalism," pp. 5-6, 8, 69.

6. Schmotter, "Ministerial Careers in Eighteenth-Century New England: The Social Context, 1700-1760," *Journal of Social History* 9 (Winter, 1975): 262-63.

7. Youngs, *God's Messengers*, pp. 66, 73; see especially chapter 4, "Congregational Clericalism," pp. 64-91.

8. Ibid., pp. 73-76.

9. The comment about the Anglican clergy appears on p. 138; the rest of this paragraph is based on Youngs' chapter 5 ("The Failure of Clericalism" and chapter 6 "Revivalism").

10. Schmotter, "Provincial Professionalism," pp. 13, 69.

11. Youngs, *God's Messengers*, p. 64.

12. Ibid., pp. 138-41.

13. Ibid., p. 138; Bushman makes essentially the same argument. See his *Puritan to Yankee, Part Four*, "Churches, 1690-1765."

14. Williston Walker, *The Creeds and Platforms of Congregationalism* (Boston, 1960), pp. 229-30. The best discussion of the Cambridge Platform a discussion that stresses its ambiguities and compromises, appears in David Hall's *Faithful Shepherd*, chapter 5.

15. Walker, *Creeds and Platforms*, p. 234.

16. When the Springfield First Church sent out its invitations to attend the ordination of Robert Breck in 1736 it sent them to the ministers rather than the local churches. The enormity of the ensuing protest provides a vivid illustration of how unusual this was. With regard to the choosing of delegates to ecclesiastical councils: Ebenezer Parkman thought that "in choosing ye delegates (for a council) the pastor usually nominates ye persons whom he would commend unto ye choice of ye chh." (Parkman, Commonplace Book, Undated entry, American Antiquarian Society.)

17. Hall, *Faithful Shepherd*, p. 219: "to the ministers the strengthening – or at least the enforcement – of Article 16 [which established the system of ecclesiastical councils – called "synods" in the Platform text] appeared imperative."

18. Harvard First Church to Nathan Stone, 27 February 1738-39, Stone Papers, Massachusetts Historical Society.

19. Report of a Council at Leominster, 26 July 1757, Nathan Stone Papers, Massachusetts Historical Society.

20. Church Records, Groveland First Church, 11 June, 14 July and 1 August 1746. The Church Records are at the church.

21. William Baldwin to Nathan Stone, 6 August 1748, Nathan Stone Papers, Massachusetts Historical Society.

22. Parkman, undated entry, Commonplace Book, Parkman Family Papers, American Antiquarian Society.

23. Josiah Cotton, Memoirs, entry for 8 January 1730 (p. 205), Josiah Cotton Papers, Massachusetts Society.

24. Ibid.

25. See, for example the minority report produced by some members of the ecclesiastical council which met at Concord in 1772. The council had apparently split 17-32 in reaching their decision (although the minority report, styled a "protest," was signed by only thirteen). The minority report (or "protest") not only gives its reasons for disagreement, but goes as far as to declare the majority report invalid and without authority, because it tends "to the destruction of order in our churches." The aggrieved brethren "had cause of complaint against the pastor of the church [and] are justifiable in their withdrawing from the communion of the church." Since "their whole management of the controversy . . . rather merits praise than deserves blame," the minority feels no hesitancy in confering their own legitimacy upon their behavior. The "Protest," dated 4 July 1772, is in the Curwen Papers, American Antiquarian Society.

26. John White, *New England's Lamentations* . . . (1734), p. 30.

27. See the single piece of paper, undated and unsigned, in vol. 2 of the Curwen Papers, American Antiquarian Society. From internal evidence, this is perhaps a copy of remarks made by Samuel Mather at the ordination of Andrew Eliot.

28. For a different interpretation of the Saybrook Platform, see Bushman, *Puritan to Yankee*, pp. 150-55.

29. Williston Walker, *Creeds and Platforms*, pp. 495-500.

30. The list of delegates and pastors appears in Ibid., p. 502.

31. Bushman, *Puritan to Yankee*, p. 151.

32. Walker, *Creeds and Platforms*, p. 503.

33. Ibid., pp. 504-5.

34. Ibid., p. 504.

35. Compare part 2, section 6 of the Proposals of 1705 (Walker, *Creeds and Platforms,* p. 489) with Article 4 of the Saybrook Platform (Walker, p. 503). Walker's note about abandonment of separate voting appears on p. 503 n.3.

36. Ibid., pp. 505-6.

37. Ibid., p. 487.

38. Ibid., p. 503 n.2.

39. Bale to Ezra Stiles, 7 January 1761, in Stiles, *Extracts from Itineraries . . .* , p. 486.

40. Devotion to Stiles, 25 April and 8 February 1768, in Stiles, *Extracts from Itineraries . . .* pp. 471-72, 472. See also Devotion to Stiles, 30. February 1769, Ibid., p. 476.

41. Edwards, *The Works of President Edwards . . .* vol. 1 (New York, 1843), p. 122.

42. Ministerial associations have been virtually ignored by historians.· The Rev. Alonzo H. Quint is the only person to have written directly on ministerial associations. See his "The Origins of Ministerial Associations in New England," *Congregational Quarterly* 2 (1860) 203-12. Youngs devoted only nine pages to the subject, although it is, obviously, central and even crucial to his argument. See Youngs' *God's Messengers,* pp. 69-78. Schmotter, although he discusses the appearance of professional attitudes among the clergy in the eighteenth century, does not undertake an examination of the ministerial associations. This is a remarkable lacuna, from the perspective of the history of the ministry in the eighteenth century, and from the perspective of the history of professionalism. Unlike the available studies of the ministry in the eighteenth century, the studies of the bar and of the medical profession both devote considerable attention to the emergence of professional organizations among their subjects. The absence of professional organizations among the New England clergy suggests, in contradiction to the existing literature, that the clergy was unable to organize itself professionally until well into the nineteenth century, and that this impotency sprang from their geographical dispersion and from their direct and complete dependence upon particular congregations.

43. The records of the "Hampshire County Association of Ministers, 1731-1747" are at the Forbes Library, Northampton, Massachusetts. The first entry is dated October 1731.

44. I derived my figures on the number of ministers settled from Harold Field Worthley, *An Inventory of the Record of the Particular (Congregational) Churches of Massachusetts Gathered 1620-1805* (Cambridge, 1970).

45. The records of the Bradford Association are at the Andover-Newton Theological Seminary, Newton, Massachusetts.

46. The records of the Plymouth Association are at the Congregational Library, Boston.

47. The records of the Boston-Cambridge Association can be found in Massachusetts Historical Society, *Proceedings*, vol. 6 (1879-80), pp. 262-81. The figures for the Salem Association are taken from Alonzo H. Quint, "Some Account of Ministerial Associations (Congregational) in Massachusetts," *Congregational Quarterly* 4 (1863): 302. Hampshire, Plymouth and Bradford Association figures from records mentioned above. Sherburne Association figures from Joseph Baxter, Notes, Massachusetts Historical Society. Marlborough Association figures from Joseph Allen, *The Worcester Association and its Antecedents*... (Boston, 1868), pp. v-vi.

48. Bradford Association records, ANTS, passim.

49. Joseph Baxter, Notes, Massachusetts Historical Society, passim.

50. Joseph Baxter, a member of the Sherburne Association, thought that association meetings were valuable because through them ministers' "hearts may be more engaged and knit to one another and their love and affection to each other may be augmented." See Baxter's *Notes*, p. 77.

51. Hampshire Association records, pp. 10, 28, 46.

52. Ibid., p. 10.

53. Ibid., pp. 37, 39.

54. Ibid., p. 46.

55. Bradford Association records, passim.

56. Plymouth Association records, passim.

57. The case is described by Clifford Shipton, *Sibley's Harvard Graduates*.

58. Hampshire Association records, p. 17.

59. See for example, William Cooper's *Reply* . . . (Boston, 1736), published anonymously. "The *Reply* looks as though its author had read John Wise . . . " (Alonzo Quint, "The Origins of Ministerial Associations . . . ," p. 210).

60. For composition of the council see William Sprague, *Annals of the American Pulpit*... vol. 1 (New York, 1859), pp. 385-86.

61. See for example, Perry Miller, *Jonathan Edwards* (1949), pp. 129-30; Clifford Shipton, *Sibley's Harvard Graduates*; Youngs' *God's Messengers*, pp. 86-87; Sprague, vol. 1, pp. 385-86. Only Quint expresses a contrary opinion: "The Association seem to have expressed no opinion upon the matter in dispute . . . Nor does it, in fact, appear, that the Association claimed any such extraordinary powers, or took

any action except as the case was brought before them by outside parties . . . . "
(Quint, "The Origins of Ministerial Associations. . . . " pp. 290-10).

62. Hampshire Association records, p. 17.

63. Youngs, "Congregational Clericalism: New England Ordinations before the Great
     Awakening," *William and Mary Quarterly* 31 (July 1974) 486. See also Young's
     God's Messengers, pp. 30-38.

64. Clifford Shipton, *Sibley's Harvard Graduates*, p. 12.

65. These figures were compiled from Shipton's *Harvard Graduates* and from the
     Bradford Association records.

66. Interestingly, the Association did discuss the matter of a replacement for Rand.
     However, this was only at the behest of a delegation from Sunderland. See
     Hampshire Association records, entry for 9 October 1745 (p. 46).

67. Plymouth Association records, 6 September 1725.

68. Hampshire Association records, 2 May 1739.

69. Hampshire Association records, 8 April 1740.

70. Ibid., 8 April 1740 and 7 April 1741.

71. Allen, *The Worcester Association and its Antecedents*, pp. 1-36.

72. Josiah Cotton, Memoirs, entry for 8 January 1748/49 (pp. 387-88), Massachusetts
     Historical Society. The documents produced by the controversy are in the Ebenezer
     Parkman Family Papers, American Antiquarian Society.

Chapter 2

1. Benjamin Colman to Robert Wodrow, 1 March 1720, in "Some Unpublished
    Letters of Benjamin Colman, 1717-1725," ed. Niel Caplan Massachusetts Historical
    Society, *Proceedings* 77 (1965) 117-19; Clifford Shipton, *Sibley's Harvard Grad-
    uates* . . . vol. 4 (Boston, 1933), pp. 304-7.

2. Coman to Wodrow, 1 March 1720, op. cit., p. 119.

3. Ibid., p. 119.

4. Ibid., p. 118.

5. Shipton, op. cit., pp. 305-6.

6. James Schmotter, "Provincial Professionalism: The New England Ministry, 1692-1745 (Unpublished Ph.D. dissertation, Northwestern University, 1973); J.W.T. Youngs, Jr., *God's Messengers: Religious Leadership in Colonial New England, 1700-1750* (Baltimore, 1976).

7. William Shurtleff, *The Gospel Ministry* . . . (Boston, 1739), p. 24; Shurtleff, *The Labor that Attends the Gospel Ministry* (Boston, 1727), p. 17; John Hancock, *A Sermon* . . . (Boston, 1726), p. 29; John Tufts, *Anti-Ministerial Objections* . . . (1725), pp. 21, 27; Thomas Clap, *The Greatness and Difficulty of the work of the Ministry* . . . (Boston, 1732), p. 10.

8. Shurtleff, *The Labor*, pp. 8-9; Solomon Williams, *The Glorious Reward of Wise and Faithful Teachers* . . . (Boston, 1730), p. 6; Charles Chauncy, *Ministers Exhorted and Encouraged* . . . (Boston, 1744), pp. 9-10; Clap, *Greatness and Difficulty*, p. 11.

9. Ibid., pp. 10-12.

10. Ibid., pp. 8-9; Nathaniel Henchman, *The Divine Pastor* . . . (Boston, 1733), p. 21.

11. Youngs, "Congregational Clericalism: New England Ordinations Before the Great Awakening," *William and Mary Quarterly* 31 (July, 1974): 481-90; Clap, *Greatness and Difficulty*, p. 10. But see also the comments on pp. 27-28 of the present study.

12. Shurtleff, *Gospel Ministry*, pp. 5-6, 20-21; Clap, *Greatness and Difficulty*, p. 20; Henchman, *Divine Pastor*, p. 3; Solomon Williams and Eleazur Wheelock, *Two Letters* . . . (Boston, 1744), as in *The Great Awakening: Documents on the Revival of Religion, 1740-1745*, ed. Richard L. Bushman (New York, 1870), p. 133.

13. Jonathan Edwards, *Works* . . . vol. 1 (1843), p. 169; Chauncy, *Ministers Exhorted*, p. 7.

14. Ibid., p. 8.

15. Edward Holyoke, *Obedience and Submission* . . . (Boston, 1737), p. 14.

16. Ebenezer Parkman, Commonplace Book, undated entry, in Parkman Family Papers, American Antiquarian Society; Nathaniel Eells, *The Evangelical Bishop* . . . (Boston 1734), pp. 32-35.

17. Ibid., p. 33; William Williams, *The Office and Work* . . . (Boston, 1729), p. 14; John Tufts, *A Humble Call* . . . (Boston, 1729), p. 16; Clap, *Greatness and Difficulty*, p. 10; Henchman, *Divine Pastor*, p. 14; John Devotion to Ezra Stiles, 14 July 1769, in Stiles, *Extracts from the Itineraries* . . . , ed. F.B. Dexter (Boston, 1916), p. 477.

18. Eliphat Adams, *The Gracious Presence* . . . (New London, 1730), p. 39.

19. Quoted by Youngs, *God's Messengers*, pp. 88-91. Youngs attributes this to the entire New England ministry.

20. Youngs, *God's Messengers*, pp. 109-41; Schmotter, "Provincial Professionalism, pp. 280-331.

21. Samuel Mather, *An Apology for the Liberties of the Churches in New England* . . . (Boston, 1738), pp. 9-10.

22. Shurtleff, *Gospel Ministry*, p. 26; Henchmen, *Divine Pastor*, p. 20; William Rand, *Superior Dignity*, p. 11; Adams, *Gracious Presence*, p. 38.

23. Niles, *Tristitle Ecclesiarum*, 11; Baster, Notes, 23 March 1703, Massachusetts Historical Society, p. 32; Ibid., 27 October 1702, p. 12.

24. Holyoke, *Obedience and Submission*, pp. 25-26; Samuel Stoddard, *Defects of Preachers Reproved* . . . (Boston, 1724), pp. 22-23; Mather, *Apology*, pp. 144-45; John White, *New England's Lamentations*... (Boston, 1734), pp. 34-35.

25. John Hancock, *Rulers Should be Benefactors* . . . (Boston, 1722), pp. 2-3; Thomas Foxcroft, *A Discourse* . . . (Boston, 1727), pp. 5-7; Mather, *Apology*, pp. 22; Benjamin Colman, *Ministers and People*... (1732), pp. 7-9.

26. Samuel Phillips' words appear as an appendix to John Barnard's *Christian Churches* . . . (Boston, 1731), p. 34; Eells, *Evangical Bishop*, pp. 33-34. Compare this statement in 1734 with his remarks five years later: "Though a minister be an officer in the Universal Church, yet he is not an officer in every particular church, but in that particular church only which is committed to his charge . . . every church has its own pastor, and every pastor his own church." Eells, *The Pastor's Introduction* . . . (1739), p. 10. Nathaniel Mather, *A Discussion of the Law-fullness* . . . (Boston, 1730), preface; John Tufts, *A Humble Call* . . . (Boston, 1729), p. 4; White, *New England's Lamentations*, pp. 31-32; Mather, *Apology*, p. 51. See also the remarks made by Josiah Cotton in 1743: "This year Mr. Daniel Rogers was ordained . . . a minister at large over no particular church, so properly an itinerant minister; and it is said that one Mr. [Bennell?] is also so ordained. God grant that these things may not run us into divisions and confusions." Josiah Cotton, Memoirs, entry for 8 January 1742/43, pp. 313-14, Cotton Papers, Massachusetts Historical Society.

27. Symms' remarks are contained in *A Particular . . . Account* . . . (Boston, 1726), pp. 60-64; Ebenezer Parkman, Commonplace Book, undated entry, Parkman Family Papers, American Antiquarian Society.

28. Benjamin Colman to Robert Wodrow, 9 Dec 1717, in "Some Letters," ed. Caplan p. 107; White, *New England's Lamentations*, p. 34; Hancock, *A Sermon* . . . (Boston, 1726), pp. 18-20; Mather, *Apology*, pp. 40-44.

29. Anon., *A Letter* . . . (Boston, 1731), p. 7; Thomas Foxcroft, *Divine Right* . . . (Boston, 1731), p. 7.

30. David Hall, *The Faithful Shepherd: A History of the New England Ministry in the Seventeenth Century* (New York, 1972, 1974), p. 95; Joseph Sewall, *Rulers Must be Just* . . . (1724), p. 23; Colman to Wodrow, 23 January 1719, in "Some Letters," p. 112.

31. Groveland First Church, Church Records, entry for 9 October 1730 (p. 102). The records are at the church.

32. Groveland Church Records, entry for 23 October 1730 (p. 103).

33. As quoted by William B. Sprague, *Annals of the American Pulpit* . . . vol. 1 (New York, 1859), p. 240. Sprague provides no date for this incident.

34. Clifford Shipton, *Sibley's Harvard Graduates* . . . vol. 10 (Boston, 1958), p. 494.

35. Sewall, *Rulers*, p. 23; Mather, *Apology*, p. 44; White, *Lamentations*, pp. 34-35.

36. Anon., *A Letter . . . Relating to the Office of Ruling Elders* . . . (Boston, 1731), p. 5; see also Anon., *Some Brief Remarks* . . . (Boston, 1731), passim; The Goddard remarks are contained in Edward Goddard's Autobiography, in Goddard Family Papers, American Antiquarian Society. Goddard and Samuel Mather, both champions of the office of ruling elders, frequently corresponded with one another on that topic. See for example, Goddard to Mather, 15 December 1740, Goddard Family Papers, American Antiquarian Society, in which Goddard acknowledges receipt of Mather's *Apology* and concurs with his opinion that ruling elders are necessary to prevent clerical tyranny.

37. Eleazur Wheelock to Joseph Clark, 23 January 1739, Wheelock Papers, Dartmouth College Archives, Dartmouth College; Benjamin Colman to Robert Wodrow, 17 November 1719, in "Some Unpublished Letters," p. 118; Colman to Wodrow, Ibid., 11 June 1723; Josiah Cotton, Memoirs, Cotton Papers, Massachusetts Historical Society, 30 January 1740/41, p. 291.

38. White, *New England's Lamentations*, p. 36; Parkman, Commonplace Book, undated entry, Parkman Family Papers, American Antiquarian Society; Mather, *Apology*, p. 20.

Chapter 3

1. Michael J. Crawford, ed., "The Spiritual Travels of Nathan Cole," *William and Mary Quarterly* 33 (January, 1976): 92-93.

2. Franklin, *Autobiography*, p. 120.

3. As quoted in Richard Bushman, ed., *The Great Awakening: Documents on the Revival of Religion, 1740-1745* (New York, 1970), pp. 22-23.

4. Jonathan Parsons, "Account of the Revival at Lyme," in Alan Heimert and Perry Miller, eds., *The Great Awakening: Documents Illustrating the Crisis and its Consequences* (Indianapolis, 1967), pp. 198-200.

5. On the morphology of the conversion process, see Perry Miller, "Preparation for Salvation in Seventeenth-Century New England," in his Nature's Nation (1967), and Darrett Rutman, *American Puritanism: Faith and Practise* (1970), pp. 97-106.

6. Crawford, "Spiritual Travels," pp. 90; Parsons, "Revival at Lyme," pp. 197-99.

7. Samuel Blair, "A Short and Faithful Narrative of the Late Remarkable Revival of Religion in the Congregation of New-Londonderry . . ." (Philadelphia, 1744), as reprinted in Bushman, *Great Awakening*, p. 76.

8. Ibid., p. 75.

9. Ibid., p. 77.

10. Theophilus Pickering, "The Rev. Mr. Pickering's Letters . . . " in Bushman, *Great Awakening*, p. 57.

11. Ibid., pp. 127-28.

12. Quoted by Clifford K. Shipton, *Biographical Sketches of Those Who Attended Harvard College in the Classes 1719-1722* (Boston), p. 440.

13. William W. Fenn, "Charles Chauncy," in *Dictionary of American Biography*, vol. 4 ed. Allen Johnson and Dumas Malone (New York, 1930), p. 43.

14. Williston Walker, "Charles Chauncy," in his *Ten New England Leaders* (New York, 1901, 1969), p. 287.

15. Ibid., p. 271.

16. Charles Chauncy, *The Only Compulsion Proper to be Made Use of in the Affairs of Conscience and Religion* . . . (Boston, 1739), p. 16.

17. Charles Chauncy, *Enthusiasm Described and Caution'd Against* . . . (Newport, 1742), p. v; Chauncy, *The Only Compulsion*, p. 15.

18. Chauncy, *The Outpouring of the Holy Ghost* . . . (Boston, 1742), p. 13.

19. Chauncy, *A Letter* . . . *to Mr. George Wishart* . . . (Edinburgh, 1742), in Bushman, *Great Awakening*, pp. 117-21.

20. Chauncy, *Enthusiasm Described*, pp. 16-17.

21. Chauncy, *Gifts of the Spirit to Ministers* . . . (Boston, 1742), pp. 7-8.

22. Chauncy, *Seasonable Thoughts* . . . (Boston, 1742), pp. 324-27, as quoted by Stow Persons, "The Cyclical Theory of History in the Eighteenth-Century," in Cushing Strout, *Intellectual History in America* Vol. 1 (New York, 1968), p. 51.

23. Chauncy, *Letter to. . . Wishart*, in Bushman, *Great Awakening*, p. 121.

24. On Edwards' appropriation of Locke, see Perry Miller, *Errand into the Wilderness* (1956), chapter 7, "The Rhetoric of Sensation." Tennent's remark was originally meant as a criticism of the Liberals. See Tennent, *The Danger of an Unconverted Ministry*, in Bushman, *Great Awakening*, p. 90.

25. Chauncy, *Letter to. . . Wishart*, in Bushman, *Great Awakening*, p. 118.

26. Chauncy, *Enthusiasm Described*, p. 15.

27. Chauncy, *Outpouring*, p. 26; Chauncy, *The New Creature* . . . (Boston, 1741), pp. 25-26; Chauncy, *The Only Compulsion*, p. 9.

28. Alan Heimert, *Religion and the American Mind* (1966), p. 92; *Enthusiasm Described*, pp. iii-iv; *Letter to. . . Wishart*, in Bushman, *Great Awakening*, p. 121.

29. Chauncy, *Seasonable Thoughts*, pp. 422-23; Leonard Labree, "The Conservative Attitude Toward the Awakening," *William and Mary Quarterly* 1 (1944): 438.

30. Heimert, *Religion*, p. 258; Chauncy to Stiles, 14 June 1771, in Ezra Stiles, *Extracts From the Itineraries. . .* (1916), pp. 450-51.

31. Perry Miller, *Johathan Edwards* (n.p., 1949), p. 178; Edwin Gaustad, *The Great Awakening in New England* (Chicago, 1957, 1967), p. 67.

32. Clifford Shipton, *Sibley's Harvard Graduates* vol. 4 (Boston, 1933), pp. 189-98.

33. Shipton, p. 194.

34. Adams, *A Discourse. . .* (1734), passim.

35. Robert G. Pope, *The Half-Way Covenant* . . . (Princeton, 1969), p. 107; Shipton, p. 190; Joshua Hempstead, "Diary," New London County Historical Society, *Colls.*, 1 (1901), entries for 17 May 1741 (p. 326), 10 and 17 October 1742 (p. 400), 1 May 1743 (p. 409), 5 August 1744, 2 and 16 September 1744 (pp. 430-31).

36. Adams, *Discourse* . . . (1734), p. 65; Adams, *Gracious Presence* . . . (1730), p. 37; Adams, *Discourse. . .* (1734), pp. 62-63.

37. Hempstead, "Diary," p. 376.

38. Ibid. For evidence of Jonathan Parsons' religious radicalism, see his *Wisdom Justified of Her Children . . .* (Boston, 1742), and Gaustad, *Great Awakening*, p. 76.

39.   Hempstead, "Diary," pp. 277-83.

40.   Ibid., pp. 379-80.

41.   Solomon Williams to Eleazar Wheelock, 17 July 1741, in Wheelock Papers, Dartmouth College Archives.

42.   Hempstead, "Diary," entries for 17 November 1741, p. 384; 26 June 1742, p. 395; 15-19 July 1742, p. 379; 30 March 1742/43, p. 407.

43.   Ibid., entries for 16 June and 10 August 1745, pp. 444 and 446-47.

44.   *The Testimony of the Pastors of the Churches* . . . (Boston, 1743); Joshua Gee, *A Letter to . . . Nathaniel Eells* . . . (Boston, 1743); Edwin S. Gaustad, *The Great Awakening in New England* (1957, 1965), pp. 63-64; Stiles, *Itineraries*, p. 414. Stiles' estimate is probably an accurate one. The "counter-convention" of New Light ministers that met in Boston in July of 1743 could get only 111 signatures to their declaration of support for the Awakening, even though it condemned the movement's excesses and though it was circulated throughout New England. This is more than signed the Old Light declaration of May 1743, but still only a little more than 1/4 of all New England ministers. Hawke's comment appears in his *In the Midst of a Revolution* (1961).

45.   Appleton, *God, Not Ministers to Have the Glory* . . . (Boston, 1741), p. 18.

46.   Ibid., p. 21.

47.   Ibid., pp. 41-42.

48.   Ibid., pp. 21-22, 43.

49.   Eliot, *The Faithful Steward* . . . (Boston, 1742), pp. 18; 19-20; 30; 34.

50.   Ibid., pp. 5-6, 11. Quoted by Clifford K. Shipton, *New England Life in the Eighteenth Century* (Cambridge, 1963), p. 405. Ibid., pp. 405-6. For Chauncy's attacks on the Baptists, see the following: *Boston Gazette*, 2 November, 14 December and 28 December of 1778; *Boston Evening-Post*, 28 November 1778; and *Independent Chronicle*, 8 and 15 October 1778.

51.   Ibid., pp. 21-22.

52.   Shipton, *Harvard Graduates*, vol. 4, pp. 352-59; James Cogswell, *Faithfulness in the Service of Christ* . . . (Norwich, 1776), p. 14.

53.   Shipton, *Harvard Graduates*, pp. 354, 357-58.

54. Edmund S. Morgan, *The Gentle Puritan: A Life of Ezra Stiles, 1727-1795* (New Haven, 1962), pp. 77, 107.

55. Ibid., pp. 74, 167, 174.

56. Stiles, *Discourse on the Christian Union* (Newport, 1761), p. 50.

57. Stiles' account of the Joseph Snow affair is related in his *Literary Diary of Ezra Stiles...* vol. 1 (New York, 1901), pp. 114-15.

58. The best short study of Hopkins' thought is Williston Walker's "Samuel Hopkins," in his *Ten New England Leaders* (New York, 1901, 1969), pp. 313-57. That Hopkins' Calvinism did not imply a disregard to human suffering can be seen in his anti-slavery work during and after the Revolution. See David S. Lovejoy, "Samuel Hopkins: Religion, Slavery and the Revolution," *New England Quarterly*, 40 (June, 1967): 227-43. Lovejoy argues that Hopkins first formulated his anti-slavery views during the Great Awakening and then "openly used the Revolutionary movement to push an attack against Negro slavery," and that he "exploited the Declaration and the Revolution to support a conviction about equality already arrived at on other grounds" (p. 227).

59. The two letters are: Chauncy to Stiles, 14 November 1769; and Chauncy to Stiles, 14 June 1771, both in Stiles, *Itineraries*, pp. 450-51.

60. Morgan, *Gentle Puritan*, p. 207.

61. These entries spanned the period from 18-30 March 1773 in Stiles, *Literary Diary*, pp. 356-57; for Stiles' conversation with the rabbi, see entries for 8 April 1773 (pp. 362-63) and 14 June 1773 (p. 386).

62. See for example, *Itineraries*, p. 67.

63. Stiles, *Christian Union*, pp. 94-95.

64. Ibid.

Chapter 4

1. Stiles as quoted by Conrad Wright, *The Beginnings of Unitarianism in America* (Boston, 1955), p. 241; Thomas Clap, *A Brief History and Vindication of the Doctrines Received and Established in the Churches of New England . . .* (New Haven, 1955), pp. 42-43; William Hart, *A Discourse Concerning . . . Regeneration . . .* (New London, 1742), p. 48; Hart, *The Hold Scriptures . . .* (New London, 1743), pp. 23-24.

2. Chauncy to Stiles, 21 July 1761, in Ezra Stiles, *Itineraries . . .* (New Haven, 1916), p. 440. Stiles discusses the pamphlet's popularity in Ibid., p. 440 n. 4.

3. On the millennialism of the Revolutionary mentality, see Alan Heimert, *Religion and the American Mind* (Cambridge, 1966), pp. 413-552; Ernest Lee Tuveson, *Redeemer Nation: The Idea of America's Millennial Role* (Chicago, 1968), chapter one; John G. Buchanan, "Puritan Philosophy of History From Restoration to Revolution," *Essex Institute Historical Collections* 104 (1968): 342-43; Nathan Hatch, "The Origins of Civil Millennialism in America: New England Clergymen, War with France, and the Revolution," *William and Mary Quarterly* 31 (July, 1974): 407-30. Stiles' remarks are found in his *Discourse on the Christian Union . . .* (Boston, 1761), pp. 101-2 and 155.

4. Samuel Webster, *A Winter-Evenings Conversation . . .* (Boston, 1757), pp. 21-22; William Smith, *A Sermon . . .* (Philadelphia, 1755), pp. 9-10, 16; Ebenezer Gay, *Natural Religion Distinguished from Revealed* (Boston, 1759), p. 15; David Rittenhouse, *An Oration . . .* (Philadelphia, 1775), p. 27.

5. Hitchcock, *Natural Religion*, p. 20.

6. Stiles, *Christian Union*, pp. 10-11; Andrew Eliot, *A Discourse on Natural Religion . . .* (Boston, 1779), pp. xxxii, xxvii-xxviii. On the Arminian notion of original sin, see Wright, *Beginnings of Unitarianism*, chapter three.

7. William Shurtleff, *The Labour that Attends the Gospel Ministry . . .* (Boston, 1757), pp. 8-9.

8. Eliot, *Natural Religion*, p. xxxi.

9. Stiles, *Christian Union*, p. 10.

10. Experience Mayhew, *Grace Defended, In a Modest Plea for an Important Truth . . .* (Boston, 1744), as reprinted in Richard Bushman, *The Great Awakening: Documents on the Revival of Religion, 1740-1745* (New York, 1970), p. 142.

11. Ibid., p. 142.

12. Jonathan Edwards, *A Treatise Concerning Religious Affections . . .* (Boston, 1746), as reprinted in Alan Heimert and Perry Miller, eds., *The Great Awakening: Documents Illustrating the Crisis and Its Consequences* (Indianapolis, 1967), pp. 518, 521.

13. Ibid., pp. 526, 535.

14. Ibid., p. 535. For a contrary, and I think misleading interpretation, see Heimert, *Religion*, pp. 38-42.

15. Hart, *Holy Scriptures*, p. 32; Hart, *Regeneration*, p. 6. See also Chauncy, *The Out-Pouring of the Holy Ghost . . .* (Boston, 1742), pp. 13-15.

16. Nathaniel Appleton, *God, and Not Ministers to Have the Glory . . .* (Boston, 1741), pp. 42-43.

17. Stiles, *Christian Union*, p. 22.

18. Joseph Bellamy, *True Religion Delineated* . . . (Boston, 1750), as reprinted in Bushman, *Great Awakening*, p. 147.

19. Ibid., pp. 150-51.

20. Ibid., pp. 150-51, 153.

21. Appleton, *God, and Not Ministers*, p. 40.

22. Appleton, *Some Unregenerate Persons Not So Far From the Kingdom of God as Others*... (Boston, 1763), pp. 4, 15.

23. Hart, *Regeneration*, pp. 10-11, 34-35.

24. Ibid., pp. 20, 28-31.

25. Ibid., pp. 21, 37.

26. Stiles, *Christian Union*, pp. 25-26.

27. Ibid., p. 20.

28. Mayhew, *Grace Defended*, in Bushman, *Great Awakening*, p. 141.

29. Ibid., pp. 138-40.

30. Perry Miller, "The Marrow of Puritan Divinity," in his *Errand into the Wilderness* (Cambridge, 1956, 1964), pp. 48-98.

31. Mayhew, *Grace Defended*, p. in Bushman, *Great Awakening*, p. 142.

32. Ibid., p. 143.

33. Ibid.

34. Bushman, *Great Awakening*, p. 133.

35. Stiles, *Christian Union*, pp. 52-53.

36. Mayhew, *Grace Defended*, in Bushman, *Great Awakening*, p. 144.

Chapter 5

1. See, for example, *A Letter from the Associated Ministers of the County of Windam*... (Boston, 1745), p. 3.

2. William Hart, *Discourse Concerning ... Regeneration ...* (New London, 1742), p. 6.

3. David McGregore, *The Spirits of the Present Day Tried ...* (Boston, 1742), p. 2.

4. David McGregore, *Christian Unity and Peace ...* (Boston, 1765), pp. 13-14.

5. McGregore, *Spirits*, p. 25; *Christian Unity*, pp. 17-18, 21, 28-29.

6. Ibid., pp. 21-23.

7. Ibid., p. 9.

8. Solomon Williams, *The Sad Tendency of Divisions and Contentions . . .* (Newport, 1751), pp. 22-24; Williams, *The True State of the Question . . .* (Boston, 1751), p. i.

9. Jack Backus' reasons for separating from the congregational church at Norwich, Connecticut, as reprinted in Richard Bushman, ed., *The Great Awakening: Documents on the Revival of Religion, 1740-1745* (New York, 1970), p. 103.

10. Edwards, "A Farewell Sermon," in Edwards, *Works ...* vol. 1 (1843), pp. 79-80.

11. Ibid., pp. 60, 115, 189.

12. Ibid.

13. Ibid., p. 86.

14. Ibid., pp. 90-92, 94, 169.

15. Ibid., pp. 96, 100, 122. For a defense of the "moral sincerity" argument, see Experience Mayhew, *Grace Defended . . .* (Boston, 1744), and Charles Chauncy, *Breaking of Bread ...* (Boston, 1772).

16. Edwards, *Works*, pp. 190-91; Miller, *New England Mind: From Colony to Province* (Boston, 1953), p. 204.

17. Williams, *The True State ...* (Boston, 1751), pp. 5-6, 139.

18. Ibid., pp. 142-44.

19. Ibid., p. 134; John Devotion to Ezra Stiles, 25 April 1768, and Chauncy Whittelsey to Stiles, 30 June 1768, both in Ezra Stiles, *Extracts from Itineraries*, pp. 474 and 491. Even Charles Chauncy voiced this fear. See his letter to Richard Price, 5 October 1772, in "The Price Papers," Massachusetts Historical Society, *Proceedings*, 2nd Series, 17 (May, 1903), 266.

20. Williams, *True State*, pp. 140-41, 5-6.

21. Chauncy, *Breaking of Bread*, p. 73.

22. Ibid., pp. 25, 35, 37-38, 43-44, 51.

23. Ibid., p. 57.

24. See for example, Richard Bushman, *From Puritan to Yankee* . . . (New York, 1967, 1970), pp. 215-17; Edwin Gaustad, *The Great Awakening in New England* (Gloucester, Mass., 1957), pp. 110-11.

25. Devotion to Stiles, 25 April 1768, in Stiles, *Itineraries*, p. 474.

26. Noah Hobart, *The Principles of Congregational Churches*... (New Haven, 1959), p. 3.

27. Hart to Stiles, 12 August 1768, in Stiles, *Itineraries* . . . , p. 496.

28. Hart, *The Holy Scriptures*... (New London, 1743), p. 17.

29. Hart to Stiles, 14 March 1769, in Stiles, *Itineraries*, p. 498.

30. Hart, *Remarks on a Late Pamphlet*... (New Haven, 1760), p. 111.

31. See Stiles, *Literary Diary*, ed. F.B. Dexter, 3 vols. (1910), passim.

32. Stiles, *Discourse on the Christian Union* . . . (Boston, 1761), pp. 48, 85.   See also Stiles, *Literary Diary*, entries for 6 February 1771 (p. 89); 3 October 1771 (p. 168); and 2 December 1771 (pp. 190-91).

33. *Christian Union*, pp. 96-97.

34. As quoted by Edmund S. Morgan, *The Gentle Puritan*... (New Haven, 1962), p. 252.

35. Madison, Federalist no. 51, as reprinted in John D. Lewis, ed., *Anti-Federalist Versus Federalist: Selected Documents* (Scranton, 1967), p. 352.

Chapter 6

1. Ebenezer Parkman, Undated entry, Commonplace Book, Parkman Family Papers, American Antiquarian Society.

2. Benjamin Colman to Robert Wodrow, 23 January 1719, in Niel Caplan, "Some Unpublished Letters of Benjamin Colman, 1717-1725," Massachusetts Historical Society, *Proceedings* 77 (1965): 114.

3. J.W.T. Youngs, Jr., *God's Messengers: Religious Leadership in Colonial New England, 1700-1750* (Baltimore, 1776), p. 73.   In Connecticut the clergy of each

county had been formed into ministerial associations by order of the Saybrook Platform of 1708.

4. Joseph Baxter, Notes, entry for 18 October 1715, in Joseph Baxter Papers, Massachusetts Historical Society.

5. Parkman, Commonplace Book, undated entry.

6. Baxter, Notes, entry for 9 May 1704, p. 77.

7. Youngs, *God's Messengers*, pp. 29-30.

8. Excepting Benjamin Flagg, who attended the Association meetings only briefly in 1736-37. See Bradford Association Records, Andover-Newton Theological Seminary.

9. For Samuel Bacheller, see an undated entry in the Church Records of the Haverhill Third Church, at the church. For Parson, see Clifford Shipton, *Sibley's Harvard Graduates*... vol. 4 (Boston, 1942), p. 393.

10. Hampshire County Ministerial Association, Record Book, Forbes Library (North-ampton), entry for 12 October 1742, p. 40.

11. Baxter, Notes, entry for 9 May 1704, p. 77.

12. Ibid., entry for 18 October 1715, p. 203.

13. Samuel Willard, circular letter to the various ministerial associations in Massachusetts, 6 November 1704, appended to the Boston/Cambridge Association Records, Massachusetts Historical Society, *Proceedings* 17 (1879-1880): 280-81.

14. Jackson Turner Main, *The Social Structure of Revolutionary America* (Princeton, 1965), p. 96.

15. Hampshire Association Records, p. 8.

16. Baxter, Notes, entry for 3 May 1709, p. 162.

17. Hampshire Association Records, p. 40.

18. Baxter, Notes, entry for 18 October 1715, Joseph Allen, *The Wooster Association and its Antecedents*... (Boston, 1868), p. 10.

19. William Rand, *The Labor That Attends the Gospel-Ministry* . . . (Boston, 1727), pp. 29-30.

20. Israel Loring, Diary, entry for 16 August, 1750, in Loring Papers, Massachusetts Historical Society.

21. Baxter, Notes, entry for 3 May 1709, pp. 162-63.

22. Ibid., entry for 18 October 1715, p. 204.

23. Bradford Association Records, entry for 3 June 1719.

24. Baxter, Notes, entry for 31 October, 1704, p. 104.

25. Hampshire Association Records, entry for 26 April 1737, p. 22.

26. Ibid., entry for 18 April 1738, p. 24.

27. Ibid., entry for 3 May 1739, p. 31.

28. "Records of the Cambridge Association," Massachusetts Historical Society, *Proceedings* 17 (1879-1880): p. 269, entry for 12 June 1693.

29. Ibid., entry for 2 August 1697, p. 275.

30. Baxter, Notes, 3 May 1709, p. 164.

31. Williston Walker, *The Creeds and Platforms of Congregationalism* (Boston, 1960), pp. 219-20, 227-29, 503.

32. Eleazur Wheelock to Noah Webster, 21 November 1737, Wheelock Papers, Dartmouth College Archives, Dartmouth College.

33. Eleazur Wheelock to Silas Woodworth, 23 July 1743, Wheelock Papers.

34. Solomon Williams to Eleazur Wheelock, 24 November 1740, Wheelock Papers.

35. Thomas Clap, *The Greatness and Difficulty of the Work of the Ministry . . .* (Boston, 1732), pp. 10-12.

36. Bradford Association Records, entry for 3 June 1719.

37. Allen, *The Worcester Association,* p. 9.

38. Hampshire Association Records, entry for October 1731, p. 1.

39. Allen, *Worcester Association,* p. 21.

40. Hampshire Association Records, October 1731, p. 1.

41. Ibid., 3 October 1732, p. 4; 9 October 1733, p. 9.

42. Allen, *Worcester Association,* p. 9.

43.   Bradford Association Records, single entry for 1740, p. 9.

44.   Ibid., entries for 17 April 1723 and 25 April 1725.

45.   Allen, *Worcester Association*, p. 22.

46.   Ibid., p. 22.

47.   Records of the Plymouth Association, entry for 8 April 1729.   The record book is
      at the Congregational Library, Boston.

48.   Bradford Association Records, entry for October 1733.

49.   Ibid., entry for 17 May 1720.

50.   Allen, *Worcester Association*, p. 11.

51.   Bradford Association Records, entry for 17 June 1730.

52.   Ibid., entry for May 1750.

53.   Hampshire Association Records, entry for 13 October 1741, p. 36.

54.   Baxter, Notes, entry for 18 October 1715, p. 204.

55.   Ibid., entry for 3 May 1709, pp. 162-64.

56.   Ibid., entry for 18 October 1715, pp. 204-5.

57.   Hampshire Association Records, entry for 13 October 1747, p. 49.

58.   Baxter, Notes, entry for 20 March 1710/11, pp. 168-69.

59.   Perry Miller, *The New England Mind: From Colony to Province* (Boston, 1953),
      p. 248.

60.   Baxter, Notes, entry for 9 May 1704, p. 75.

61.   Hampshire Association Records, entries for 12 October 1736, 28 October 1746 and
      13 October 1747.

62.   "Records of the Cambridge Association," entry for 5 September 1692, p. 268.

63.   Baxter, Notes, entries for 20 October 1713 and 22 June 1714.

64.   Hampshire Association Records, entries for 18 April 1738, 12 April 1743, 18
      October 1743, and 17 April 1744.

65. Samuel Niles, *Tristitalae Ecclesiarum...* (Boston, 1745), pp. 15-19.

66. "Records of the Cambridge Association," entry for 4 April 1692, p. 267.

67. Bradford Association Records, entry for 21 June 1720.

68. Hampshire Association Records, entries for 28 October 1746 and 13 October 1737, pp. 49-50.

69. Jonathan Edwards to Joseph Sewall and Thomas Prince, April 1751, in Curwen Papers, American Antiquarian Society.

70. The composition and results of the council at Northampton, which met on 22 June 1750, are in Edwards, *Works...*, vol. 1 (New York, 1843), pp. 81-82.

71. Baxter, Notes, entry for 9 May 1704, p. 76.

72. John White, *The Gospel Treasure in Earthen Vessels...* (Boston, 1725), p. 33.

73. Baxter, Notes, entry for 21 March 1704, pp. 70-74.

74. Ibid., entry for 9 May 1704, pp. 75-77.

75. Anon., *A Letter to the Clergy...* (New York, 1760), p. 21

76. Eleazur Wheelock to Capt. Joseph Clark, 23 January 1739, Wheelock Papers.

77. As quoted in Alan Heimert and Perry Miller, eds., *The Great Awakening: Documents Illustrating the Crisis and its Consequences* (Indianapolis, 1967), p. 510.

78. Baxter, Notes, entry for 9 May 1704, p. 75.

79. Zabdiel Adams, *The Happiness and Pleasure of Unity...* (Boston, 1772), p. 16.

80. Baxter, Notes, entry for 9 May 1704, p. 76.

81. Jonathan Stebbins to Eleazur Wheelock, 13 April 1743, Wheelock Papers.

82. Ebenezer Parkman, The Diary of Ebenezer Parkman (Worcester, 1974), entries for 22 January and 11 June 1745, pp. 110, 119.

83. Quoted by Clifford Shipton, *Sibley's Harvard Graduates* vol. 10 (Boston, 1958), p. 350.

84. Parkman, Diary, entries for 9 and 10 March 1745, p. 115.

85. Baxter, Notes, entry for 18 October 1715, pp. 204-05.

86.   Ezra Stiles, *Discourse on the Christian Union...* (Boston, 1761). pp. 95, 115.

Chapter 7

1.   On the revival of interest in millennial thinking, see David Smith, "Millennarian Scholarship in America," *American Quarterly* 17 (1965): 535-49; and Ernest Tuveson, *Redeemer Nation: The Idea of America's Millennial Role* (Chicago, 1968), pp. vii-xi and 232-34. The remark about America being "raised up . . . " was made by Ezra Stiles in his *The U.S. Elevated to Honor and Glory . . .* , 2nd ed. (Worcester, 1785), pp. 62-53 and 70. Heimert's remark is from his *Religion and the American Mind* (Cambridge, 1966), p. 21.

2.   Heimert, *Religion,* p. 354; Nathan Hatch, "The Origins of Civil Millennialism in America: New England Clergymen, War with France, and the Revolution," *William and Mary Quarterly* 31 (July, 1974): 429; McLoughlin, "The American Revolution as a Religious Revival: the Millennium in One Country," *New England Quarterly* 40 (March, 1967): 99-110.

3.   Heimert, pp. 354-55, Hatch, "Origins. . . ." passim; McLoughlin, "American Revolution. . . . " pp. 105-6, 108-10.

4.   Stiles, *Discourse...* (1761), pp. 101-2.

5.   Edwards, *Works.*... vol. 1 (Worcester, 1843), pp. 47-48.

6.   Ibid., pp. 49-50; C.C. Goen, "Jonathan Edwards: A New Departure in Eschatology," *Church History* 28 (1959): 25.

7.   Earnest Tuveson, *Millennium and Utopia: A Study in the Background of the Idea of Progress* (New York, 1949, 1964), pp. ix-xi.

8.   Ibid., p. ix.

9.   Miller, "The End of the World," in his *Errand into the Wilderness* (Cambridge, 1956), pp. 233-39. For a refutation of Miller's view, see C.C. Goen, "Jonathan Edwards," pp. 36-37.

10.   *Works,* vol. 1 pp. 426-29.

11.   Ibid., pp. 482-83.

12.   Ibid., pp. 491-94.

13.   *Thoughts on the Revival of Religion in New England . . .* (1740), in *Works,* vol. 3 pp. 314-15.

14.   Heimert, *Religion,* pp. 62-64; Hatch, "Origins," pp. 414-17.

15. Stiles, *U.S. Elevated*, pp. 96-98, 116-19. For Stile's various computations of the millennium, see Edmund S. Morgan, *The Gentle Puritan* . . . (New Haven, 1962), p. 162: Abiel Holmes, *The Life of Ezra Stiles* . . . (Boston, 1798), p. 139: and Stiles, *U.S. Elevated*, p. 118. Stiles articulated his millennial vision most fully in *The U.S. Elevated*, first published in 1783. But his numerous references to a golden age in the 1760s and 1770s make it evident that he had entertained such a vision much earlier.

16. *U.S. Elevated*, pp. 70, 96-98, 119.

17. Ibid., pp. 97-116.

18. Stiles, *Discourse on the Christian Union* . . . (Boston, 1761), p. 101.

19. Ibid., pp. 95-96, 155.

20. Ibid., pp. 95, 125. Stiles assumed that Congregationalists and Presbyterians agreed on the scriptural validity of presbyterian ordination, and he made it a condition of union in the *Discourse*. See especially pp. 30-32, 37; *U.S. Elevated*, 101-9; and *Literary Diary* . . . ed. F.B. Dexter, 1910, entries for 9 October 1771 and 2 December 1771 (pp. 171, 190-91). On Stiles' attitude toward the Separatists, Baptists, and Quakers, see diary entries for 16 July 1771 and 9 October 1771 (pp. 122, 170-71), and *Christian Union*, pp. 27, 95.

21. *Christian Union*, pp. 102-3, 112, 114, 110-15; *U.S. Elevated*, pp. 98, 116-17.

22. *Christian Union*, pp. 38, 66-67, 79, 96.

23. *Literary Diary*, vol. 1 entries for 3 October 1771 and 6 February 1771 (p. 89, 168).

24. *Christian Union*, pp. 101-2.

25. Morgan, *Gentle Puritan*, p. 218. Stiles, *Itineraries*, 8, 17, 49-50, 92, 109, 114, 137. *Literary Diary*, vol. 1 entries for 4 June 1770, 23 January 1771 and 17 August 1772 (pp. 54, 85-86, 266-67).

26. Ibid., vol. 1 entries for 23 June 1771, 6 August 1771, and 17 August 1772, (pp. 85-86, 134-35, 266-68).

27. *Literary Diary*, vol. 1 entry for 19 February 1773 (p. 345).

28. *Christian Union*, p. 96.

Bibliography

Contemporary Books and Pamphlets

Adams, E. *A Sermon Preached at Windham, July 12, 1721* . . . (New London: T. Green) 1721.

_____ (1677-1753). *The Gracious Presence of Christ with the Ministers of the Gospel*... (New London: T. Green) 1730.

_____. *A Discourse*... (New London: T. Green) 1734.

Anon. *A Vindication of an Association from the Charge of Countenancing Heresy in Doctrine and of Partiality in Conduct* . . . *Written at the Desire of the Association, by one of their number*... (Portsmouth N.H.: D. Fowle) 1758.

_____. *A Sermon on Natural Religion*... *By a Natural Man* (Boston: I. Thomas) 1771.

_____. *A Reply to Some Remarks on a Letter to a Gentlemen Relating to the Office of Ruling Elders* (Boston: No publisher) 1731.

_____. *A Letter* . . . *Relating to the Office of Ruling Elders* . . . (Boston: No publisher) 1736.

_____. *Some Brief Remarks*... (Boston: T. Fleet) 1731.

_____. *A Letter to a Gentleman Relation to the Office of Ruling Elders in the Church* (Boston: No publisher) 1731.

Appleton, Nathaniel. *God, and not Ministers to have the Glory of all success Given to the Preached Gospel*... (Boston: G. Rogers & D. Fowle) 1741.

_____. *Some Unregenerate Persons Not so Far from the Kingdom of God as Others*... (Boston: S. Kneeland) 1763.

Backus, Isaac. *A Church History of New England* . . . vol. II (Providence, R. I.: John Carter) 1784.

Barnard, John. *Christian Churches*... (Boston: B. Green) 1731.

_____. *The Lord Jesus Christ the Only* . . . *A Sermon* . . . *to the Assembly of Ministers at Their Anniversary Convention in Boston* . . . *June 1, 1738* . . . (Boston: S. Kneeland & T. Green) 1738.

_____ (1681-1770). *The Throne Established by Righteousness* . . . (Boston: No publisher) 1734.

_____. *The True Divinity of Jesus Christ, Evidenced in a Discourse at the Public Lecture in Boston*... *July 16, 1761*... (Boston: Edes & Gill) 1761.

Barnard, Thomas. *Ordination Sermon*... (Boston: J. Draper) 1762.

Bayley, Abner (1716-1798). *The Duty of Ministers to Preach not Themselves, but Jesus Christ*... (Portsmouth: Daniel Fowle) 1764).

_____. *The Promises through Christ* . . . *Two Sermons Preached at Salem, N.H.* ... *Nov. 28, 1779*... (Newbury: John Mycall) 1780.

Bellamy, Joseph. *True Religion Delineated*... (Boston: S. Kneeland) 1750.

Blair, Samuel. "Revival of Religion at New-Londonderry . . . " *The Christian History for 1744* . . . (William Bradford) 1744.

Briant, Lemuel. *Letter to Mr. Porter* . . . (Boston: J. Green) 1750.

Brown, Moses. *The Scripture Bishop, or, the Divine Right of Presbyterian Ordination and Government* . . . (Boston: No publisher) 1733.

Cabot, Marston (1705-1756). *The Nature of Religious Thanksgiving* . . . (S. Kneeland & T. Green) 1735.

_____. *The Nature of Religious Fasting Opened in two short discourses* . . . (Boston: Printed for John Eliot) 1734.

Caldwell, John. *An Impartial Trial of the Spirit Operating in this Part of the World* . . . (Williamsburg: William Parks) 1746.

_____. *An Impartial Trial of the Spirit Operating in this Part of the World* . . . (Boston: T. Fleet; William Parks) 1742; 1746.

A Caveat Against Unreasonable and Unscriptural Separations. In a Letter sent FM a Minister to some of his Brethren . . . (Boston: No publisher) 1748.

Champion, Judah. *A Brief view of the Distresses, Hardships, and Dangers our ancestors encountered in settling New England* . . . (Hartford: Green & Watson) 1770.

Chauncy, Charles. *The Benevolence of the Diety* . . . (Boston: Powars & Willis) 1784.

_____. *The Breaking of Bread* . . . (Boston: Printed for Thomas Leverett) 1772.

_____. *Enthusiasm Described and Cautioned Against* . . . (Newport: J. Draper) 1742.

_____. *Gifts of the Spirit to Ministers* . . . (Boston: Rogers & Fowle) 1742.

_____. *A Letter to the Reverend Mr. George Whitefield* . . . (Boston: Rogers & Fowle) 1745.

_____. *Ministers Cautioned* . . . (Boston: Rogers & Fowle) 1744.

_____. *Ministers Exhorted and Encouraged to take Heed to Themselves and to Their Doctrine* . . . (Boston: Rogers & Fowle, for S. Eliot) 1744.

_____. *The New Creature* . . . (Boston: G. Rogers) 1741.

_____. *The Only Compulsion Proper to be made use of in the Affairs of Conscience and Religion* . . . (Boston: J. Draper) 1739.

_____. *The Outpouring of the Holy Ghost* . . . (Boston: T. Fleet) 1742.

_____. *Seasonable Thoughts* . . . (Boston: Rogers & Fowle) 1743.

Choate, Col. John (1697-1765). *Col. Choate's Reasons of Dissent from the Judgment of a Council* . . . (Portsmouth: D. Fowle) 1760.

_____. *Remarks on the Late Printed Answer to Colonel Choate's Reasons* . . . (Boston: Edes & Gill) 1761.

Clap, Thomas. *The Answer of the Friend in the West, to a Letter from a Gentlemen in the East entitled, The Present State of the Colony of Connecticut Considered* . . . (New Haven: James Parker) 1755.

_____. *The Answer of the Friend in the West, to a Letter from a Gentlemen in the East* . . . (New Haven: James Parker) 1755.

_____. *A Brief History and Vindication of the Doctrines received and established in the Churches of New England* (New Haven: James Parker) 1755.

_____. *The Greatness and Difficulty of the Work of the Ministry* . . . (Boston, John Eliot 1732).

Clark, Peter. *The Advantages and Obligations Arising from the Oracles of God Committed to the Church and its Ministry* . . . (Boston: J.Draper) 1745.

Cleveland, Aaron. *A Letter to the Rev. Mr. Foxcroft, being an Examination of his Apology for the Rev. Mr. Whitefield* . . . (Boston, J. Fleet) 1745.

Colman, Benjamin. *Faithful Pastors Angels of the Churches* . . . (Boston: J. Draper) 1739.

_____ (1673-1747). *Government the Pillar of the Earth* . . . (Boston: Printed for T. Hancock) 1730.

_____. *The Merchandise of a People Holiness to the Lord*... (Boston: J. Draper) 1739.

_____. *Ministers and People under special Obligations to Sanctity, Humility and Gratitude; for the Great Grace given them in the Preached Gospel* . . . (Boston: S. Kneeland & T. Green, for S. Gerish) 1732.

_____. *Righteousness and Compassion The Duty and Character of Pious Rulers* . . . (Boston: J. Draper) 1736.

_____. *The Unspeakable Gift of God*... (Boston: J. Draper) 1739.

_____. *The Wither'd Hand Stretched Forth at the Command of Christ, and Restored*... (Boston: J. Draper) 1739.

Cotton, John. *Ministers of the Gospel should Speak, Not as Pleasing Men, but God, who tries their Hearts*... (Boston: B. Green) 1734.

_____ (1712-1789). *Seasonable Warning to these Churches* . . . (Boston: S. Kneeland & T. Green) 1746.

_____. *Seasonable Warning to These Churches. A Narrative of the Transactions at Middleborough*... (Boston: S. Kneeland & T. Green) 1746.

_____. *The Way of the Congregational Churches Cleared* (London: Mathew Simmons for John Bellamie) 1648.

Davies, Samuel. *Religion and Public Spirit*... (Philadelphia: James Hatton) 1755.

Douglas, William (1691-1752). *A Summary, Historical and Political, of the First Planting*... (Boston: Rogers & Fowle) 1747.

Eastham, Massachusetts. South Church. *A Church of Christ Vindicated. A Short and Plain Relation of some Transactions in the South Church at Eastham* . . . (Boston: No publisher) 1724.

Eells, Nathaniel (1677-1750). *The Evangelical Bishop. A Sermon Preached at Stonington, in Connecticut Colony, June 14th, 1733, at the Ordination of the Reverend Mr. Nathaniel Eells* ... (New London) 1734.

_____. *The Ministers of God's Word must Approve Themselves unto God* . . . (Boston: No publisher) 1725.

_____. *The Ministers of the Gospel, as Ambassadors for Christ, should beseech men to be Reconciled to God*... (Boston: No publisher) 1729.

_____. *The Pastor's Introduction and Charge. A Sermon Preached at Middletown in Connecticut Colony*... (New London: T. Green) 1739.

Eliot, Andrew. *A Discourse on Natural Religion* . . . (Boston: Printed by D. Kneeland, for Nicholas Bowes) 1771.

_____. *The Faithful Steward*... (Boston: Tho. Fleet for Samuel Eliot) 1742.

_____. *An Inordinate Love of the World Inconsistent with the Love of God* . . . (Boston: Rogers & Fowle, for S. Eliot) 1744.

Eliot, Jared. *Give Ceasar his Due. Or, the Obligation that Subjects are Under to their Civil Rulers*... (New London: T. Green) 1738.

_____. *The Two Witnesses: Or, Religion Supported by Reason and Divine Revelation*... (New London: T. Green) 1736.

Enfield, William (1741-1797) *Biographical Sermons* . . . (Philadelphia: Francis Bailey & T. Lang) 1791, and (Boston: T. Hall) 1794.

Fiske, Samuel (1689-1770). *The Character of the Candidates for Civil Government, especially for Council*... (Boston: T. Fleet) 1731.

Fitch, Jabez. *A Plea for the Ministers of New England* (Boston: Printed for Samuel Gerrish) 1724.

_____. *Gospel Ministers Considered under the Similtude of Fathers of Men* . . . (Boston: S. Kneeland & T. Green) 1732.

Foxcroft, Thomas. *Some Seasonable Thoughts on Evangelic Preaching* . . . *Occasioned by* the late visit and Uncommon Labours ... of ... Whitefield ... (Boston: Rogers & Fowle, for S. Eliot) 1740.

_____. An Apology in Behalf of the Reverend Mr. Whitefield ... (Boston: Rogers & Fowle) 1745.

_____. "Appendix" to Jonathan Edwards, An Humble Inquiry ... (Boston: S. Kneeland) 1749.

_____. Humilis Confessio: The Saints United Confession, in Disparagement of their own Righteousness ... (Boston: No publisher) 1750.

_____. The Importance of Ministers ... (Boston: Printed for D. Henchman) 1728.

_____. A Discourse Preparatory to the Choice of a Minister ... (Boston: Printed by Gamaliel Rogers) 1727.

_____. The Divine Right of Deacons ... (Boston: B. Green, for D. Henchman & J. Phillips) 1731.

_____. A Practical Discourse Relating to the Gospel Ministry ... (Boston: Printed for Nicholas Buttolph) 1718.

_____. Ministers, Spiritual Parents ... (Boston: Printed for S. Gerrish) 1718.

Gale, Benjamin. The Present State of Connecticut ... (New London: T. Green) 1755.

_____. A Reply to a Pamphlet Entitled the Answer of the Friend ... (New London: T. Green) 1755.

Gay, Ebenezer. Natural Religion, as Distinguished from Revealed ... (Boston: John Draper) 1759.

_____. The Alienation of Affections from Ministers Considered and Improved ... (Boston: Rogers & Fowle) 1747.

Gee, Joshua. A Letter ... to Nathaniel Eells ... (Boston: J.Draper for N. Procter) 1743.

Hall, Samuel (1695-1776). The Legislature's Right, Charge and Duty in Respect of Religion ... (New London: T. Green) 1746.

Hall, Willard (1703-1779). An Answer to "Colonol Choate's Reasons of Dissent ... " (Boston: Edes & Gill) 1761.

Hancock, John (1671-1752). A Sermon Preached at the Ordination of Mr. John Hancock ... (Boston: Printed for Thomas Hancock) 1726.

_____. An Expostulatory and Pacific Letter ... (Boston: Rogers & Fowle) 1743.

_____. Rulers Should be Benefactors ... (Boston: B. Green) 1722.

Hart, William. Remarks on a Late Pamphlet ... (New Haven: J. Parker & Co.) 1760.

_____. The Holy Scriptures the Compleat and only Rule of Religious Faith and Practice ... (New London: T. Green) 1743.

_____. A Discourse Concerning the Nature of Regeneration ... (New London: T. Green) 1742.

_____. (1713-1784). A Scriptural Answer to the Question, viz What are the Necessary Qualifications for a Lawful and Approved Attendance on The Sacraments of the New Covenant (New London: T. Green) 1772.

_____. The Holy Scriptures Compleat and Only Rule ... (New London: T. Green) 1743.

_____. A Discourse Concerning the Nature of Regeneration ... (New London: T. Green) 1742.

Haven, Samuel. Preaching Christ the Great Business of the Gospel Ministry ... (Portsmouth: D. Fowle) 1760.

Haynes, Joseph (-1800). The Priests Lips Should Keep Knowledge ... (Portsmouth: D. Fowle) 1760.

Henchman, Nathaniel. The Divine Pastor ... (Boston: S. Kneeland & T. Green for D. Henchman) 1733.

Hitchcock, Gad. Natural Religion ... (Boston: T. & J. Fleet) 1779.

Hobart, Noah. *A Congratulatory Letter from a Gentlemen in the West, to his Friend in the East*... (New Haven: James Parker) 1755.

_____ (1706-1773). *An Attempt to Illustrate and Confirm the Ecclesiastical Constitution of the Consociated Churches in the Colony of Connecticut* . . . (New Haven: B. Mecom) 1765.

_____. *The Principles of Congregational Churches*... (New Haven: James Parker) 1758.

Holyoke, Edward (1689-1769). *Integrity and Religion to be Principally Regarded, by such as Design Others to Stations of Publick Trust*... (Boston: J. Draper for J. Eliot) 1736.

_____. *Obedience and Submission to the Pastoral Watch and Rule Over the Church of Christ*... (Boston: T. Fleet) 1737.

_____. *The Duty of Ministers of the Gospel to Guard Against the Pharisaism and Sadducism, of the Present Day* . . . *Preached to the Convention of Ministers of* . . . *Massachusetts*... *May 28, 1741*... (Boston: T. Fleet for D. Henchman and J. Eliot) 1741.

Hunn, Nathanael (1708-1749). *The Welfare of a Government Considered. A Sermon* . . . (New London: T. Green) 1747.

Huntington, Enoch. *A Sermon Preached at East-Haddam, at the Ordination of the Rev. Mr. Elijah Parsons*... (New London: T. Green) 1773.

Langdon, Samuel. *The Excellency of the Word of God, in the Mouth of a Faithful Minister*... (Portsmouth: Daniel Fowle) 1756.

A Letter from the Associated Ministers of the County of Windham... (Boston: J. Draper) 1745.

A Letter to the Clergy of the Colony of Connecticut from an Aged Layman of said Colony... (New Haven: No publisher) 1760.

Locke, Samuel. *A Sermon Preached before the Ministers of the Providence of the Massachusetts*... (Boston: R. Draper) 1772.

Lord, Joseph. *The Great Priviledge of Children of God*... (Boston: B. Green) 1731.

Loring, Israel (1682-1772). *Ministers Insufficient of Themselves Rightly to Discharge the Duties of Their Sacred Calling*... (Boston: Tho. Fleet for D. Henchman) 1742.

_____. *Private Christians Helpers of their Ministers in Christ Jesus* . . . (Boston: No publisher) 1735.

_____. *The Duty of an Apostatizing People*... (Boston: S. Kneeland) 1737.

Lowell, John (1704-1767). *Ministers of the Gospel to be Cautious of Giving Offense and Concerned to Preserve their Character as Ministers of God* . . . (Boston: J. Draper for S. Kneeland & T. Green) 1739.

McGregore, David. *The Spirits of the Present Day Tried* . . . (Boston: D. Fowle for D. Henchman) 1742.

_____. *Christian Unity and Peace Recommended* . . . (Boston: W. McAlpine & J. Fleming) 1765.

Mather, Nathaniel. *A Discussion of the Lawfulness of a Pastor's Acting as an officer in other Churches Besides that which he is specially called to take the oversight of* . . . (Boston: T. Fleet) 1730.

Mather, Samuel. *The State of Religion in New England*... (Glasgow: No publisher) 1742.

_____. *An Apology for the Liberties of the Churches in New England: To Which is Prefixed A Discourse Concerning Congregational Churches* . . . (Boston: T. Fleet for D. Henchman) 1738.

Mayhew, Experience. *Grace Defended*... (Boston: B. Green for D. Henchman) 1744.

Mayhew, Jonathan. *Striving to Enter in at the Straight Gate* . . . (Boston: R. Draper, Edes & Gill, T. & J. Fleet) 1761.

_____. *Seven Sermons*... (Boston: Rogers & Fowle) 1749.

_____. *A Discourse*... (Boston: Edes & Gill, R. Draper) 1755.

Morton, Ebenezer. *More Last Words to These Churches. In Answer to* . . . [John Cotton's Seasonable Warning...]... (Boston: T. Fleet) 1746.

Niles, Samuel. *Thristitlae Ecclesiarum, or A Brief and Sorrowful Account of the Present State of the Churches in New England...* (Boston: J. Draper) 1745.

_____ (1674-1762). *Tristitlae Ecclesiarum or, A Brief Account of the Present State of the Churches in New England...* (Boston: J. Draper) 1745.

Parsons, Jonathan. *Wisdom Justified of Her Children . . .* (Boston: Rogers & Fowle for N. Procter) 1742.

Prince, Thomas. *A Chronological History of New England . . .* (Boston: Kneeland & Green for S. Gerrish) 1736.

_____. *A Sermon Delivered... At His [Own] Ordination...* (Boston: J. Franklin) 1718.

_____. *The Dying Prayer of Christ . . .* (Boston: S. Kneeland and T. Green for S. Gerrish) 1732.

_____. *The People of New England...* (Boston: B. Green for D. Henchman) 1730.

_____. *Civil Rulers Raised up by God...* (Boston: Printed for Samuel Gerrish) 1728.

_____. *Annals of New England . . .* vol. 2, no. 1 (Boston: S. Kneeland, and J. & T. Leverett) 1754.

Rand, William. *Gospel-Ministers should be Chiefly Concerned to Please God and Not Men, in the Discharge of their Office...* (Boston: Green & Russell) 1757.

_____. *The Ministers of Christ are to Enrich Those They Minister Unto . . .* (Boston: T. Fleet for D. Henchman) 1741.

_____. *Ministers Should have a Sincere and Ardent Love to the Souls of their People...* (Boston: J. Fleet) 1742.

_____. *The Superior Dignity of the Office of the Ministers of Jesus Christ . . .* (Boston: John Draper) 1956.

_____. *Ministers must Preach Christ Lord, and Themselves Servants . . .* (Boston: S. Kneeland & T. Green) 1736.

Reasons for Adhering to our Platform, as a Rule of Church-Government, and Objections Against Ruling Elders Answered... (Boston: No publisher) 1734.

Sewall, Joseph. *A Day of Prayer, to Seek to God for the More Plentiful Effusion of His Holy Spirit...* (Boston: D. Fowle for D. Henchman) 1742.

_____. *Christ Victorious . . . By the Light of His Preached Gospel . . .* (Boston: S. Kneeland & T. Green) 1733.

_____. *Nineveh's Repentance...* (Boston: J. Draper for D. Henchman) 1740.

_____. *Rulers Must be Just...* (Boston: B. Green) 1724.

Shurtleff, William. *The Obligations upon all Christians to Desire and Endeavour the Salvation of others...* (Boston: T. Fleet for D. Henchman) 1741.

_____. *The Labour that Attends the Gospel-Ministry* (Boston: B. Green) 1727.

_____. *Gospel Ministers Exhibited Under the Notion of Stars and our Lord Jesus Christ as Holding these Stars in his Right Hand . . .* (Boston: J. Draper for D. Henchman) 1739.

Slater, Richard. *A Sermon Preached Before the Gen. Assembly of the Col. of Conn. . . . May 12th, 1768...* (New London: T. Green) 1768.

Smith, William. *A Sermon, Preached in Christ-Church, Philadelphia: Before the . . . Free and Accepted Masons...* (Philadelphia: B. Franklin & D. Hall) 1755.

Some Brief Remarks, Upon a Letter to a Gentleman, Relating to the Office of Ruling Elders... (Boston: No publisher) 1731.

Stiles, Ezra. *The United States Elevated to Honor and Glory . . .* (2nd edition, Worcester: Isiah Thomas) 1785.

_____. *A Discourse on Saving Knowledge Delivered at the Installment of the Reverend Samuel Hopkins...* (Newport: Solomon Southwick) 1770.

_____. *Discourse on the Christian Union...* (Boston: Edes & Gill) 1761.

Stiles, Isaac (1697-1760).   *A Prospect of the City of Jerusalem . . . A Sermon Preached . . . May 13th, 1741 . . .* (New London: T. Green) 1742.

_____.   *The Declaration of the Assoc. of the Co. of New-Haven . . . 1744-5, concerning . . . Whitefield . . . & the State of Religion at this Day . . .* (Boston: T. Fleet) 1745.

_____.   *The Declaration of the Association of the County of New Haven . . .* (Boston: T. Fleet) 1745.

Stoddard, Solomon.   *An Appeal to the Learned . . .* (Boston: B. Green) 1709.

_____.   *The Defects of Preachers Reproved in a Sermon . . .* (New London: T. Green) 1724.

_____.   *The Duty of Gospel-Ministers . . .* (Boston: Printed for Samuel Phillips) 1718.

Stone, Nathanael.   "The Rev. Mr. Stone's Questions and Advice to the Reverend Mr. Whitefield," in *The Sentiments and Resolution of an Association of Ministers Convened at Weymouth, Jan 15th, 1744/45 . . .* (Boston: T. Fleet) 1745.

The Testimony and Advice of an Assembly of Pastors . . . July 7, 1743 . . . (Boston: No publisher) 1743.

The Testimony of the Pastors of the Churches in the Province of the Massachusetts-Bay . . . May 25, 1743 . . . (Boston: S. Kneeland & T. Green) 1743.

Thomson, John.   *The Government of the Church of Christ, and the Authority of Church Judicatories Established on a Scripture Foundation: and the Spirit of Rash Judging Arraigned and Condemned . . .* (Philadelphia: Andrew Bradford) 1741.

Tufts, John.   *Anti-Ministerial Objections . . .* (Boston: B. Green, Jr.) 1725.

_____.   (-1750).   *A Humble Call to Archippus; or, the Pastor Exhorted . . .* (Boston: Printed for S. Gerrish) 1729.

Turner, Charles.   *Gospel Directions* (Newport: A. Franklin & S. Hall) 1762.

Webb.   *A Brief Discourse at the Ordination of a Deacon . . .* (Boston: B. Green for D. Henchman & J. Phillips) 1731.

Webster, Samuel.   *Winter Evening's Conversation upon the Doctrine of Original Sin . . .* (Boston: Green & Russell) 1757.

White, John.   *New England's Lamentations . . .* (Boston: T. Fleet) 1734.

_____.   (1677-1760).   *The Gospel Treasure . . .* (Boston: No publisher) 1725.

Willard, Samuel.   *Brief Directions . . . For the Study of the Ministry . . .* (Boston: J. Draper for T. Hancock) 1735.

Williams, Elisha (1694-1755).   *Divine Grace Illustrious . . .* (New London: T. Green) 1728.

_____.   *A Seasonable Plea for the Liberty of Conscience . . .* (Boston: S. Kneeland & T. Green) 1744.

Williams, Solomon.   *The Glorious Reward of Wise and Faithful Teachers . . .* (Boston: Printed for John Eliot) 1730.

_____.   *A Firm and Immoveable Courage to Obey God, and an Inflexible Observation of the Laws of Religion the Highest Wisdom and Certain Happiness of Rulers. . .* (New London: T. Green) 1741.

_____.   (1700-1776).   *The Glorious Reward . . .* (Boston: Printed for John Eliot) 1730.

_____.   *The True State of the Question . . .* (Boston: S. Kneeland) 1751.

_____.   *The More Excellent Way. Or, the Ordinary Renewing, and Sanctifying Graces, of the Holy Spirit . . .* (New London: T. Green) 1742.

_____.   *The Sad Tendency of Divisions and Contentions in Churches . . .* (Newport: James Franklin) 1751.

_____, and Eleazar Wheelock.   *Two Letters . . .* (Boston: Kneeland & Green) 1744.

Williams, William (1688-1760).   *The Office and Work of Gospel-Ministers, and the Duty of a People Towards them, Considered in a Sermon Preached at Sutton, October 15, 1729 . . .* (Boston: No publisher) 1729.

Manuscripts

Baxter, Joseph. Notes. MHS.
Bradford Association of Ministers, Recordbook, 1719-1740. Andover-Newton Theological
    Seminar, Newton, Mass.
Colman, Benjamin. Papers, MHS.
Cotton, Josiah. Memoirs. MHS.
Curwen Papers, AAS.
Foxcroft, Thomas. Foxcroft Papers, Princeton University Library, Princeton University.
Goddard, Edward. Autobiography, AAS.
Groveland [Massachusetts] First Church. Church Records, 1727-1887. At the Church.
Hampshire County Association of Ministers. Record Book, 1731-1747. Forbes Library,
    Northampton, Massachusetts.
Loring, Israel. Diary, MHS.
Stone, Nathan. Papers, MHS.
Parkman, Ebenezer. Commonplace Book, in Francis Parkman Papers, MHS.
Plymouth Association of Ministers, Recordbook, 1721-1736, Congregational Library, Boston.
Wheelock, Eleazur. Wheelock Papers, Dartmouth College Library.
Williams, Stephen. Diary, MHS.

Collections of Contemporary Documents

Bumsted, J. M., ed. *The Great Awakening: The Beginnings of Evangelical Pietism in
    America* (Waltham: Blaisdell Publishing Co.) 1970.
Bushman, Richard L., ed. *The Great Awakening: Documents on the Revival of Religion,
    1740-1745* (New York: Atheneum) 1970.
Cambridge Association of Ministers, "Records of the Cambridge Association [of Minis-
    ters]," MHS, *Proceedings* 17 (1879-1880).
Caplan, Niel. "Some Unpublished Letters of Benjamin Colman, 1717-1725," MHS,
    Proceedings 77 (1965), 101-42.
Edwards, Jonathan. *The Works of President Edwards . . .* vols. 1-4. (New York: Leavitt)
    1843.
Goen, C.C., ed. The *Works of Jonathan Edwards . . .* vols. 1-4. (New Haven: Yale
    University Press) 1972.
Heimert, Alan and Perry Miller, eds. *The Great Awakening Documents Illustrating the
    Crisis and its Consequences* (Indianapolis: Bobbs–Merrill) 1967.
Hempstead, Joshua. "Diary," New London County Historical Society, *Collections* 1
    (1901), passim.
Lovejoy, David S., ed. *Religious Enthusiasms and the Great Awakening* (Englewood
    Cliffs: Prentice-Hall) 1969.
McLoughlin, William, G., ed. *Isaac Backus on Church, State, and Calvinism: Pamphlets,
    1754-1789* (Cambridge: Belknap Press) 1968.
Parkman, Ebenezer. *The Diary of Ebenezer Parkman.* Edited by Francis G. Walett
    (Worcester: American Antiquarian Society) 1974.
"The Price Papers," MHS, *Proceedings* 2nd series, 17 (May, 1903), 262-378.
Rutman, Darrett B., ed. *The Great Awakening: Event and Exegesis* (New York: Wiley) 1970.
Stiles, Ezra. *Literary Diary . . .* Edited by F.B. Dexter (New York: C. Scribner's Sons) 1910.
_____. *Literary Diary.* Edited by F.B. Dexter (Boston: Yale University Press) 1916.
_____. *Extracts from Itineraries, with Selections from his Correspondence.* Edited by
    F.B. Dexter (Boston: Yale University Press) 1916.

Walker, Williston. *The Creeds and Platforms of Congregationalism* (Boston: Pilgrim Press) 1960.

Secondary Works

Allen, Joseph. *The Worcester Association and its Antecedents* . . . (Boston: Nichols and Noyes) 1868.

Baldwin, Alice. *The New England Clergy and the American Revolution* (Durham: Duke University Press) 1928.

Bernhard, Harold E. *Charles Chauncy: Colonial Liberal, 1705-1787* (Chicago: Chicago University Press) 1948.

Buchanan, John G. "Puritan Philosophy of History from Restoration to Revolution." *Essex Institute of Historical Collections* 104 (1968), 329-48.

Bumsted, J.M. "Presbyterianism in 18th century Massachusetts: The Formation of a Church at Easton, 1752." *Journal of Presbyterian History* 46 (1968), 243-53.

_____. "A Caution to Erring Christians: Ecclesiastical Disorder on Cape Cod, 1717-1738." *Williams and Mary Quarterly* 28 (1971), 413-38.

_____. "Revivalism and Separatism in New England: The First Society of Norwich, Connecticut as a Case Study." *William and Mary Quarterly* 24 (1967), 588-612.

Bushman, Richard L. *From Puritan to Yankee: Character and the Social Order in Connecticut, 1690-1765* (Cambridge: Harvard University Press) 1967.

Christie, Francis. "The Beginnings of Arminianism in New England." *Papers of the American Society of Church History* 2nd series, 3 (1912), 152-72.

Clark, Joseph, S. *A Historical Sketch of the Congregational Churches in Massachusetts, 1620-1858* (Boston: Congregational Board of publication) 1858.

Cowing, Cedric, B. *The Great Awakening and the American Revolution: Colonial Thought in the 18th Century* (Chicago: Rand McNally) 1971.

Crawford, Michael J., ed. "The Spiritual Travels of Nathan Cole." *William and Mary Quarterly* 33 (January, 1976), 89-126.

Dexter, Franklin B. *Biographical Sketches of the Graduates of Yale College, 1701-1815.* 6 vols. (New York: H. Holt & Co.) 1885-1912.

Essex North Association. *Contributions to the Ecclesiastical History of Essex County, Massachusetts* (Boston: Congregational Board of publication) 1865.

Felt, Joseph B. *The Ecclesiastical History of New England* 2 vols. (Boston: Congregational Library Association) 1855-1862.

Gaustad, Edwin. *The Great Awakening in New England* (Chicago: Quadrangle Books) 1968.

Gay, Peter. *A Loss of Mastery: Puritan Historians in Colonial America* (Berkeley: University of California Press) 1966.

Goen, C.C. "Jonathan Edwards: A New Departure in Eschatology." *Church History* 28 (American Society of Church History, 1959), 25-40.

_____. *Revivalism and Separatism in New England: Strict Congregationalists and Separate Baptists in the Great Awakening* (New Haven: Yale University Press) 1962.

Goodwin, Gerald. "The Myth of 'Arminian-Calvinism'." *New England Quarterly* 41 (1968), 213-37.

Hall, David. *The Faithful Shepherd: A History of the New England Ministry in the Seventeenth-Century* (New York: Norton & Co) 1974, 1972.

Haroutunian, Joseph. *Piety Versus Moralism: The Passing of the New England Theology* (New York: H. Holt & Co.) 1932.

Hatch, Nathan. "The Origins of Civil Millennialism in America: New England Clergymen, War with France, and the Revolution." *William and Mary Quarterly* 31 (July, 1974), 407-30.

Heimert, Alan. *Religion and the American Mind* (Cambridge: Harvard University Press) 1966.

Holmes, Abiel. *The Life of Ezra Stiles . . .* (Boston: Printed by Thomas & Andrews) 1798.

Howe, Daniel Walker. "The Decline of Calvinism: An Approach to its Study." *Comparative Studies in Society and History* 14 (June, 1972), 306-27.

Jacobson, Alf E. "The Congregational Clergy in Eighteenth Century New England" (Ph.D. dissertation, Harvard University) 1962.

Jones, B.L. "Charles Chauncy and the Great Awakening in New England" (Ph.D. dissertation, Duke University) 1958.

Labaree, Leonard. "The Conservative Attitude Toward the Awakening." *William and Mary Quarterly* 1 (1944), 331-42.

Lucas, Paul R. *Valley of Discord: Church and Society Along the Connecticut River, 1936-1725* (Hanover: University Press of New England) 1976.

McLoughlin, William G. *Isaac Backus and the American Pietistic Tradition* (Boston: Little Brown) 1967.

_____. "Isaac Backus and the Separation of Church and State in America." *American Historical Review* 72 (1968), 1392-1413.

_____. *New England Dissent, 1630-1833: The Baptists and the Separation of Church and State.* 2 vols. (Cambridge: Harvard University Press) 1971.

_____. "The American Revolution as a Religious Revival." *New England Quarterly* 40 (March, 1967), 99-110.

Miller, Perry. *Errand into the Wilderness* (Cambridge: Belknap Press of Harvard University Press) 1956.

_____. *Jonathan Edwards* (New York: W. Sloane Associates) 1949.

_____. *Nature's Nation* (Cambridge: Belknap Press of Harvard University Press) 1967.

_____. *The New England Mind: From Colony to Province* (Cambridge: Belknap Press of Harvard University Press) 1953.

_____. *The New England Mind: The Seventeenth Century* (Cambridge: Belknap Press of Harvard University Press) 1939.

Mills, Frederick V. "Anglican Expansion in Colonial America, 1761-1775." *Historical Magazine of the Protestant Episcopal Church* 39 (1970), 315-24.

MiddleKauff, Robert. *The Mathers: Three Generations of Puritan Intellectuals, 1596-1728* (New York: Oxford University Press) 1971.

Morgan, Edmund S. *The Gentle Puritan: A Life of Ezra Stiles* (New Haven: Yale University Press) 1962.

_____. *Visible Saints: The History of a Puritan Idea* (New York: New York University Press) 1963.

Niebuhr, Richard. *The Kingdom of God in America* (Chicago, 1937).

Parkes, H.B. "New England in the Seventeen-Thirties." *New England Quarterly* 3 (1930), 397-419.

Persons, Stow. "The Cyclical Theory of History in the Eighteenth Century." in Cushing Strout, ed., *Intellectual History in America* (New York, 1968), 47-63.

Pope, Robert G. "New England Versus the New England Mind: The Myth of Declension." *Journal of Social History* 3 (1969-1970), 95-108.

_____. *The Half-Way Covenant . . .* (Princeton: Princeton University Press) 1969.

Quint, Alonzo H. "Some Account of Ministerial Associations (Congregational) in Massachusetts." *Conregational Quarterly* 4 (1863), 293-308.

_____. "The Origins of Ministerial Associations in New England." *Congregational Quarterly* 2 (1860), 203-12.

Rutman, David. *American Puritanism: Faith and Practise* (New York: Lippincott) 1970.

Schmotter, James. "Ministerial Careers in Eighteenth Century New England: The Social Context, 1700-1760." *Journal of Social History* 9 (Winter, 1975), 249-67.

_____. "Provincial Professionalism: The New England Ministry, 1692-1745" (Ph.D. dissertation, Northwestern University) 1973.

Shipton, Clifford K. *New England Life in the Eighteenth Century* (Cambridge: Belknap Press of Harvard University Press) 1963.

_____. "The New England Clergy of the 'Glacial Age'." *Proceedings of the Colonial Society of Massachusetts,* 32 (1933), 24-54.

Sibley, John L. and Clifford K. Shipton. *Biographical Sketches of Graduates of Harvard College,* 17 vols. (Boston: Massachusetts Historical Society) 1965.

Sklar, Robert. "The Great Awakening and Colonial Politics: Connecticut's Revolution in the Minds of Men." *Connecticut Historical Society Bulletin* 27 (1963), 81-95.

Smith, David. "Millennarian Scholarship in America." *American Quarterly* 17 (1965), 535-49.

Sprague, William B. *Annals of the American Pulpit . . .* Vol. 1 (New York: R. Carter) 1859.

Stout, Harry. "The Great Awakening in New England Reconsidered: The New England Clergy." *Journal of Social History* 8 (1974-75), 21-47.

Tracy, Joseph. *The Great Awakening: A History of the Revival of Religion in the Time of Edwards and Whitefield* (Boston: Tappan & Dennet; New York: Dayton & Newman) 1841 and 1842.

Trumbull, Benjamin. *A Complete History of Connecticut* (New Haven: Maltby, Goldsmith & Co.) 1818.

_____. *A Complete History of Connecticut, Civil and Ecclesiastical . . .* 2nd edition., 2 vols. (New London: H. D. Utley) 1898.

Tucker, Louis L. *Puritan Protagonist: President Thomas Clap of Yale College* (Chapel Hill: University of North Carolina Press) 1962.

Tuveson, Ernest Lee. *Millennium and Utopia: A Study in the Background of the Idea of Progress* (Berkley: University of California Press) 1949.

_____. *Redeemer Nation: The Idea of America's Millennial Role* (Chicago: University of Chicago Press) 1968.

Walker, Williston. *Ten New England Leaders* (New York: Silver, Burdett & Co.) 1901.

Winslow, Ola. *Meetinghouse Hill, 1620-1783* (New York: Macmillan) 1952.

Wright, Conrad. *The Beginnings of Unitarianism in America* (Boston: Starr King Press) 1955.

Youngs, J.W.T. "Congregational Clericalism: New England Ordinations before the Great Awakening." *William & Mary Quarterly* 31 (July, 1974), 481-90.

_____. *God's Messengers: Religious Leadership in Colonial New England, 1700-1750* (Baltimore: Johns Hopkins University Press) 1976.

Ziff, Larzar. *Puritanism in America: New Culture in a New World* (New York: The Viking Press) 1973.

Index